**FLOYD CLYMER'S MOTORCYCLIST'S LIBRARY**

# The Book of the
# NORTON "DOMINATOR" TWINS

A useful and practical maintenance handbook for owners of all 1955-65 O.H.V. vertical twins except the 1955-65 250, 350 cc lightweight models

BY
**W. C. Haycraft**

## ANNOUNCEMENT

By special arrangement with the original publishers of this book, Sir Isaac Pitman & Son, Ltd., of London, England, we have secured the exclusive publishing rights for this book, as well as all others in THE MOTORCYCLIST'S LIBRARY.

Included in THE MOTORCYCLIST'S LIBRARY are complete instruction manuals covering the care and operation of respective motorcycles and engines; valuable data on speed tuning, and thrilling accounts of motorcycle race events. See listing of available titles elsewhere in this edition.

We consider it a privilege to be able to offer so many fine titles to our customers.

**FLOYD CLYMER**
Publisher of Books Pertaining to Automobiles and Motorcycles
2125 W. PICO ST.                    LOS ANGELES 6, CALIF.

## INTRODUCTION

Welcome to the world of digital publishing ~ the book you now hold in your hand, while unchanged from the original edition, was printed using the latest state of the art digital technology. The advent of print-on-demand has forever changed the publishing process, never has information been so accessible and it is our hope that this book serves your informational needs for years to come. If this is your first exposure to digital publishing, we hope that you are pleased with the results. Many more titles of interest to the classic automobile and motorcycle enthusiast, collector and restorer are available via our website at www.VelocePress.com. We hope that you find this title as interesting as we do.

## NOTE FROM THE PUBLISHER

The information presented is true and complete to the best of our knowledge. All recommendations are made without any guarantees on the part of the author or the publisher, who also disclaim all liability incurred with the use of this information.

## TRADEMARKS

We recognize that some words, model names and designations, for example, mentioned herein are the property of the trademark holder. We use them for identification purposes only. This is not an official publication.

## INFORMATION ON THE USE OF THIS PUBLICATION

This manual is an invaluable resource for the classic motorcycle enthusiast and a "must have" for owners interested in performing their own maintenance. However, in today's information age we are constantly subject to changes in common practice, new technology, availability of improved materials and increased awareness of chemical toxicity. As such, it is advised that the user consult with an experienced professional prior to undertaking any procedure described herein. While every care has been taken to ensure correctness of information, it is obviously not possible to guarantee complete freedom from errors or omissions or to accept liability arising from such errors or omissions. Therefore, any individual that uses the information contained within, or elects to perform or participate in do-it-yourself repairs or modifications acknowledges that there is a risk factor involved and that the publisher or its associates cannot be held responsible for personal injury or property damage resulting from the use of the information or the outcome of such procedures.

## WARNING!

One final word of advice, this publication is intended to be used as a reference guide, and when in doubt the reader should consult with a qualified technician.

# Preface

NORTON single-cylinder O.H.V. motor-cycles (dealt with in another Pitman maintenance handbook) and the O.H.V. vertical twins covered in this maintenance handbook all have a world-wide reputation for a good engineering and external finish, quick acceleration, ability to maintain high average speeds, stamina and tenacious road-holding qualities. Undoubtedly many years of factory participation in major road races such as the T.T. have greatly helped in the progressive development of Norton motor-cycles with these very desirable qualities.

The 500 cc Model 88, introduced in 1953 and available up to 1963, proved to be a big success and has been followed by an attractive and improved range of "Dominator" models whose engines are all of similar basic design with cubic capacities varying from 500 to 750 cc. This range has included Standard, De Luxe, and Sports Special (SS) models. The present range of three models combines good looks with an above-average performance.

This handbook contains *all* essential *maintenance* instructions, and also much useful advice on overhauling, applicable to the following Norton "Dominator" Twins:

1. The 1955–63 497 cc Model 88 (Standard, De Luxe).
2. The 1962–5 497 cc Model 88SS (Sports Special).
3. The 1956–62 597 cc Model 99 (Standard, De Luxe).
4. The 1962 597 cc Model 99SS (Sports Special).
5. The 1962–3 646 cc Model 650 (Standard, De Luxe).
6. The 1962–5 646 cc Model 650SS (Sports Special).
7. The 1964–5 745 cc "Atlas."

Note that where instructions given in this book are not dated or do not have sub-headings referring to specific Norton models, they are applicable to *all* of the models specified above. Many of the instructions dealing with the 1965 Models 88SS, 650SS, and the "Atlas" apply also to the 1966 versions of these three powerful and fast Nortons, but some technical modifications affecting maintenance are probable during 1966. It is now the policy of Norton Motors Ltd. to make such alterations progressively at any time during the year instead of simultaneously at the end of the

## PREFACE

year as hitherto. Most of the 1955 instructions also apply to the 1949–54 Model 7, but this machine had a standard type Amal carburettor, an oil pressure gauge, etc.

The primary purpose of this handbook is to assist *you* to keep your Norton "Dominator" mechanically efficient, to reduce its running costs to the minimum, and to minimize its annual depreciation. A well maintained Norton has, subject to careful riding, a considerably greater expectation of life than one which is maintained in a casual manner or neglected, and it gives far more pleasure to its owner.

In conclusion I sincerely thank Norton Villiers Ltd. of North Way, Walworth Industrial Estate, Andover, Hants. and also Amal Ltd. and Joseph Lucas Ltd. of Birmingham for supplying much technical data and for kindly allowing me to reproduce many excellent copyright illustrations of practical value.

W. C. H.

# Contents

1. HANDLING YOUR NORTON . . . . . . . 1
   Starting-up procedure—Running-in

2. THE AMAL CARBURETTOR . . . . . . . 6
   Adjustments and faults—Carburettor maintenance

3. NORTON LUBRICATION . . . . . . . . 14
   Engine lubrication—The motor-cycle parts

4. THE LIGHTING SYSTEM (MAGNETO IGNITION) . . . . 30
   Dynamo maintenance (1949–57)—The alternator and rectifier (1962–5 models)—Care of the battery (1949–65)—Lucas lamps and horns (1955–65)—The wiring circuit

5. THE LIGHTING SYSTEM (COIL IGNITION) . . . . . 50
   The system explained—Use of system—Maintenance of lighting–ignition system

6. GENERAL MAINTENANCE . . . . . . . 58
   Repairs and spares—Cleaning, etc.—Sparking plugs and magnetos—Valve clearances—Decarbonizing and valve grinding—Miscellaneous engine overhaul—Care of chains—The oil-bath chaincase—The clutch—The gearbox—Front and rear brakes—Wheels and tyres—Steering head adjustment—Front and rear suspension

*Index* . . . . . . . . . . . 119

# 1 Handling your Norton

**See that Your Riding Position is Good.** To obtain maximum control and minimum fatigue while riding a sporty Norton "Dominator" Twin it is most important to have a good riding position.

If the riding position on your mount is unsuitable you can alter the positions of the handlebars, the handlebar controls, and the footrests as required. The handlebar position can readily be altered after slackening its four securing bolts, and clip fittings enable the positions of the handlebar levers to be adjusted to suit the handlebar angle. It is also possible to vary considerably the positions of the footrests and the foot gear-change lever. Where desirable, the position of the rear-brake pedal can on many Nortons be altered by means of an adjustable brake-pedal stop.

**The Lighting Switch.** On all Norton heavyweight twins the lighting switch positions (magneto and coil models) are as follows:

OFF: Headlamp bulbs, tail lamp, speedometer, and sidecar lamps (where fitted) switched off.

L: Headlamp pilot bulb, tail lamp, speedometer, and sidecar lamps (where fitted) switched on.

H: Headlamp main bulb, tail lamp, speedometer, and sidecar lamps (where fitted) switched on.

**Starting-up Procedure.** The procedure for starting-up a Norton vertical twin engine is as follows:

1. Turn on the petrol tap by pulling out the knurled circular knob.

2. Verify that the foot gear-change pedal is in the "neutral" position (i.e. between first and second gears) by noting if the rear wheel can readily be rotated with the motor-cycle on its rear or centre stand, or by observing the gear indicator where fitted.

3. On a 1958–63 coil-ignition model turn the ignition key in the top of the headlamp switch *clockwise* to the "IGN" position. If the battery is run down, turn the ignition key *anti-clockwise* to the "EMG" (emergency) position (*see* page 51).

4. On a magneto-ignition model with handlebar ignition lever (i.e. on some early 1962 Model 88SS Nortons) move the ignition lever so that it is mid-way between the full advance and full retard position.

5. Open the throttle very slightly by turning the twist-grip *inwards* about one-eighth of an inch (as measured at the rim of the twist-grip rubber).

6. If the engine is *quite cold*, close the air lever completely. If it is *thoroughly warm*, open the air lever fully or nearly fully. If the engine is only *slightly warm*, open the air lever about one-third to one-half.

7. Should the engine be quite cold, momentarily depress the tickler on the carburettor float-chamber, but do not flood the carburettor so that petrol begins to drip from the float chamber. An over-rich mixture will render starting very difficult. Where twin carburettors are provided, depress both ticklers momentarily.

8. Turn the engine over sharply by applying a long swinging kick on the kick-starter pedal. Provided the engine is in sound mechanical condition

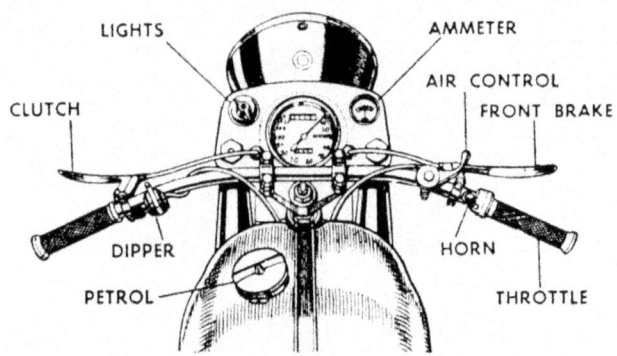

Fig. 1. The Hand Controls (1955–7 De Luxe Models)

On the Standard Models 88, 99 a panel for the lighting switch and speedometer is not provided. The ignition cut-out button is below the dualseat on the near-side, or on the magneto contact-breaker cover (1957 models).

it should fire at the first or second attempt. If it does not do so, try starting with a slightly larger throttle opening. The most satisfactory setting varies on different engines and is soon determined by practical experience. Note that starting a coil-ignition model with the ignition key in the "EMG" position usually requires more effort than is the case where the ignition key is in the normal "IGN" position.

9. As soon as the engine fires, progressively open the air lever until it is fully open, and if the ignition key on a coil-ignition model with a run-down battery has been turned to the "EMG" position for starting, immediately turn it clockwise to the "IGN" position. This is important to avoid damaging the contacts of the contact-breaker and also spoiling the condenser. On an early 1962 magneto-ignition model with manual control of the ignition, *fully advance* the ignition lever.

Adjust the throttle opening to give a moderately fast tick-over. Do not allow the engine to run slowly and do not permit it to run at very fast revolutions. Also avoid running the engine for more than a few minutes with the machine stationary. Cease warming up the engine as soon as it reaches its normal running temperature. To prevent the dangerous accumulation of carbon-monoxide fumes, always keep the lock-up or garage doors *wide open* when warming up the engine. Carbon-monoxide fumes are odourless but can be lethal, hence their danger.

10. Before riding away remove the filler cap from the oil tank and note whether oil is issuing as it should do from the oil return-pipe orifice. If the motor-cycle has been left standing for some time, the oil should return

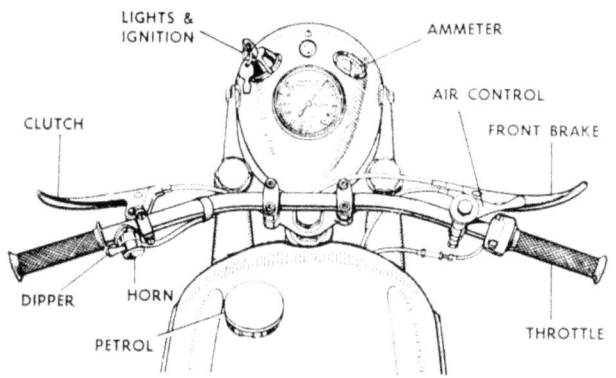

FIG. 2. THE HAND CONTROLS (1958–65 MODELS)

Where magneto ignition is provided a lighting switch replaces the combined lighting and ignition switch, and a cut-out button is fitted on the handlebars. A few Model 88 Sports Specials have an ignition lever on the left hand side of the handlebars.

in a constant stream. After a short interval the return side of the oil pump scavenges the oil sump of all oil and the flow becomes intermittent.

**Stopping Engine.** On machines with magneto ignition close the throttle and depress the ignition cut-out button on the handlebars or, on 1955-7 Models 88, 89, beneath the dualseat or on the contact-breaker cover. On coil-ignition models close the throttle and switch off the ignition by turning the key on top of the lighting and ignition switch *anti-clockwise* to the "OFF" position. The key should be in line with the motor-cycle. When parking a coil-ignition model always leave the machine with the ignition switch turned off and the ignition key removed.

It is advisable to close the petrol tap if you leave the machine standing for more than a few minutes with the engine stopped. Should petrol pass down the inclined induction pipe because of a flooding carburettor, it will cause oil dilution and accelerate wear of the engine.

**To Prevent Theft.** When parking your machine, make use of the thief-proof locking device if fitted. On all machines of recent manufacture a lock is incorporated in the handlebar lug. Every new machine is supplied with two keys.

On the earlier models an abutment on the bottom left-hand side of the steering head, and a hole in the near-side of the fork crown, permit a padlock to be fitted so as to lock the steering on full right lock. On early models with no anti-theft device, fit a padlock and chain over one of the tyres and rims.

**Correct Use of the Brakes.** Do not acquire the habit of using the rear brake only, as some riders do. Use *both* brakes simultaneously.

## RUNNING-IN

**Do Not Spoil a Good Engine.** If you have bought a brand new Norton "Dominator" or a good second-hand mount with a reconditioned engine you should nurse the engine *very* carefully during the first 1,000 miles. Neglect to run-in a new or reconditioned engine properly is likely to impair its efficiency *permanently*. Remember that piston temperature is the all-important point, and this depends not so much on road speed as on the actual throttle openings used. Excessive speed, however, is undesirable even with small throttle openings.

Engine bearing surfaces when new appear to be dead smooth, but such is not actually the case. New surfaces are covered with fine tool-marks which are quite invisible to the naked eye. Until these tool marks are eradicated and a mirror-like gloss and hardness spreads all over the piston and cylinder bore surfaces, local friction is apt to occur and the vital oil film may break down at one or more places.

Proper running-in means *progressively* increasing the load imposed on the engine, and the avoidance of excessive throttle openings and piston speed. To obtain the best results during the important running-in period of 1,000 miles also observe the following advice:

1. See that the engine, gearbox, and machine are correctly lubricated. After covering about 250 miles drain the oil from the tank and engine sump, and clean the filters. Change the oil in the gearbox after covering 500 miles. Detailed lubrication instructions are given in Chapter III.

2. Keep the engine running as lightly as possible by making full use of the gearbox, but do not allow the engine to run too fast in the lower gears. Always aim at keeping its heat down.

3. Avoid permitting the engine to tick-over for more than a few minutes with the motor-cycle stationary.

4. Do not allow the engine to labour by running too slowly in top gear or through failing to change down to a lower gear in good time when hill climbing. This applies particularly where a sidecar is attached. After climbing a steep hill close the throttle and open the air lever wide on the other side. This will cool the engine.

5. When you have covered several hundred miles check the valve

clearances, the contact-breaker gap, and the adjustment of the brakes, primary chain, secondary chain, clutch, and steering head. Some initial bedding down always occurs. Also check for tightness the various external nuts and bolts, especially those on the cylinder head and cylinder block.

6. Until at least 500 miles have been covered do not use more than one-quarter to one-third full throttle and do not ride at a speed exceeding about 50 m.p.h. on the level. At this speed the throttle should be not more than about one-eighth open.

7. After covering 500 miles assist the bedding-down of the piston thrust-faces and engine bearings by undertaking short bursts at moderate speed. Increase gradually the duration of these speed bursts until your "Dominator" will stand fairly large throttle openings for longer periods, but avoid using full throttle on the level or on hills until about 1,500 miles have been covered.

**If Piston Seizure Occurs.** If the engine is run for an excessive period during running-in with the throttle opened too wide, piston seizure may occur; this is indicated by loss of power and gradual slowing up. Do not mistake these symptoms for pre-ignition. To prevent serious piston seizure, immediately declutch, close the throttle, and allow the engine to cool for several minutes. If this is done a serious seizure may be avoided and the pistons after cooling will usually become free automatically.

If a serious piston seizure does occur the cylinder block should be removed at the first opportunity and the cylinder bores and pistons examined for scoring. Slight scoring of the piston skirts can sometimes be overlooked, and the same applies to very slight score marks on the cylinder bores. But if the cylinder bores have numerous and deep scores, reboring and the fitting of oversize pistons and rings will be necessary. Slight scoring of pistons can usually be eradicated by a good mechanic who will ease down high spots and remove slight smearing.

**During Running-in.** Norton Motors Ltd. recommend the mixing of a running-in compound containing colloidal graphite with the *engine oil* in the proportions of *one pint per gallon of oil*. This forms a graphoid surface on all working parts, prevents metal pick-up, and assists cooling. The valves also benefit. The compound is obtainable from all Norton dealers and from most garages. If used after running-in, reduce the quantity used by one half.

**Two Sound Tips.** All owners of powerful Norton "Dominator" Twins should: (1) always wear a crash helmet while riding; (2) read and thoroughly digest the contents of *The Highway Code*, published by H.M. Stationery Office, and obtainable from booksellers.

# 2 The Amal carburettor

ALL 1955 and subsequent models are provided with Amal "monobloc" type carburettors which are most reliable and require little maintenance. Some "Dominators" are fitted with twin "monobloc" instruments. The carburettor settings recommended by Norton Motors Ltd. (*see* page 8) have been carefully selected to ensure good all-round performance and a low fuel consumption. They should therefore *not be altered*. Do not try and save petrol by fitting a smaller size main jet, or jets where twin carburettors are used.

Occasionally it may be necessary to make a slow-running adjustment to ensure that the engine ticks-over correctly when the throttle twist-grip is closed. This adjustment (*see* below) is quite simple. About every 5,000 miles it is desirable to remove any foreign matter collected in the carburettor float-chamber and in the main-jet cover nut. When a very considerable mileage has been covered remove, dismantle, inspect and thoroughly clean the entire carburettor.

### ADJUSTMENTS AND FAULTS

**Slow-running Adjustment (Single Carburettor).** On "monobloc" type carburettors the adjustment should be made with the engine already *warmed up*. If slow-running is poor, screw home the pilot air-adjusting screw (*see* Fig. 3) and then unscrew it until the engine idles at an excessive speed with the throttle twist-grip fully closed and the throttle valve abutting the throttle-stop screw. The air lever should be *fully* open.

Referring to Fig. 3, unscrew the throttle-stop screw (*30*) until the engine slows up and begins to falter. Now screw the pilot air-adjusting screw (*29*) in or out as required to enable the engine to run regularly and faster. To *weaken* the mixture, screw the pilot air-adjusting screw *outwards*.

Slowly lower the throttle-stop screw until the engine again begins to falter. Then reset the pilot air-adjusting screw to obtain good and even slow-running. If after making this second adjustment the engine ticks-over too fast, repeat the adjustment a third time. The combined adjustment is quite simple in practice. It is important to avoid excessive richness of the slow-running mixture, especially if much riding is undertaken on small throttle openings. If the mixture is too rich considerable running on the pilot jet will occur, with consequently a high fuel consumption.

Aim at obtaining the best even tick-over at a *moderate speed*. Too slow a tick-over is not recommended as this can cause insufficient lubrication of the pistons and cylinder bores while the engine is hot. An excessively fast tick-over should also be avoided as this is liable to cause overheating besides excessive noise.

**Slow-running Adjustment (Twin Carburettors).** The procedure for correcting poor slow-running where twin carburettors are fitted is somewhat different to that required for a single carburettor. With the engine *warm* first disconnect one of the H.T. leads and remove the sparking plug. When doing this be sure that there is no grit or dirt inside the sparking plug recess in the cylinder head, otherwise it may enter the cylinder bore. Now start up the engine on the other cylinder and with the pilot air-adjusting screw and the throttle-stop screw obtain an even but very slow tick-over. If you begin with the pilot air-adjusting screw well closed, engine speed will increase as the screw is screwed outwards. Progressively reduce speed with the throttle-stop screw until a moderate tick-over speed is obtained.

Repeat the foregoing procedure on the other cylinder and then try running the engine on both cylinders. Tick-over may then be found to be too fast. Reduce tick-over speed by unscrewing both throttle-stop screws a similar amount. The engine is now running with both throttle valves resting on their throttle stops. Should there be an unequal amount of backlash in the short throttle cables between the carburettor mixing chambers and the cable junction-block, the engine will not accelerate properly.

Stop the engine and carefully set the adjusters on top of the mixing-chamber caps so that there is just a trace of backlash on closing the throttle twist-grip. Afterwards it is advisable to tape the adjusters with thin strips of insulation tape to prevent their moving through vibration. Although they are not so important, provided that they move to the fully open position, it is advisable to adjust the two cables for the air valves in a similar manner. Afterwards check that both throttle valves reach the fully open position and set the mid-way adjuster for the single throttle cable to provide a trace of backlash at the throttle twist-grip. Adjust the twist-grip friction to suit your individual requirements.

**Persistent Poor Slow-running.** If poor slow-running persists after making a careful slow-running adjustment as previously described, the cause may be one or more of the following:
1. An obstructed pilot jet.
2. Air leaks caused through a poor joint between the Amal carburettor flange and spacer on the cylinder head (1962 models with downdraught heads) or between the carburettor flange(s) and the induction manifold on all other models with single or twin carburettors.
3. Air leaks caused by worn inlet-valve guides.
4. Weakening of the mixture through badly seating valves.

5. Sparking plugs which have become dirty or oily, have an incorrect gap between their electrodes, or are of unsuitable type.
6. An incorrect contact-breaker gap.
7. Incorrect ignition timing.
8. Excessive carbon deposits on the pistons and combustion chambers.

**Obstructed Pilot Jet ("Monobloc" Carburettor).** The pilot jet has a very narrow fuel passage and can easily become choked. Referring to Fig. 3, to remove the pilot jet (*9*), remove its cover nut (*11*) and then unscrew the jet itself. Clean it thoroughly and then blow through it, using the motor-cycle pump. It is also important to see that the pilot by-pass (*8*) to the pilot jet (*9*) is unobstructed. This should also be blown through. The same applies to the adjacent pilot outlet.

TABLE I

AMAL CARBURETTOR SETTINGS FOR 1955–65 "DOMINATORS"

| Norton Model | Main Jet | Pilot Jet | Throttle Valve | Needle Groove |
|---|---|---|---|---|
| 88,* 88SS* (1955–65) | 240 | 30 | $3\frac{1}{2}$ | 2 |
| 99* (1956–61) | 250 | 25 | 3 | 3 |
| 650 (1962–3; one carb) | 320 | 25 | 3 | 2 |
| 650SS (1962–5; twin carb) | 250 | 25 | $3\frac{1}{2}$ | 3 |
| 750 "Atlas" (1964–5; twin carbs) | 420 | 20 | 3 | 3 |

* Where twin carburettors are fitted to these models no alteration to the carburettor settings given above is necessary. If you run a Model 88, 88SS or a Model 99 continuously on full throttle for long distances, increase the main jet size to 260 or 270 respectively.

KEY TO FIGS. 3, 4

1. Mixing-chamber cap
2. Mixing-chamber lock-ring
3. Mixing chamber
4. Jet-needle clip
5. Throttle valve (slide)
6. Jet needle (tapered)
8. Pilot by-pass
9. Pilot jet
11. Pilot-jet cover nut
12. Main-jet cover nut
13. Main jet
14. Main-jet holder
15. Needle-jet
16. Jet block
17. Air valve (slide)
18. Locking spring for 2
21. Tickler
22. Banjo bolt
23. Banjo
24. Nylon filter
25. Needle seating
26. Float-chamber needle
27. Float (hinged)
28. Float-chamber cover screws
29. Pilot air-adjusting screw
30. Throttle-stop screw
37. Float chamber
38. Float-chamber cover
39. Locating screw for 16
40. Fibre seal

THE AMAL CARBURETTOR 9

**Abnormally High Fuel Consumption.** Sometimes fuel consumption remains high in spite of the carburettor or carburettors being carefully tuned for slow-running. There are many possible causes. Some are: leakage from the carburettor due to sticking of the moulded-nylon float needle (*see* page 11); a faulty float; a poor float-chamber cover joint; a slack main-jet holder; a slack main-jet cover nut; a loose pilot jet; a worn needle-jet; slack petrol pipe union nuts; poor engine compression caused by badly fitting piston rings or pitted valves; binding of the brake shoes on the brake drums; or a slipping clutch. A careful investigation of the cause should be made.

Some less obvious reasons for a high fuel consumption are: running with incorrect valve clearances or weak valve springs; air leaks due to a poor joint between the carburettor flange(s) and inlet manifold or cylinder-head spacer; worn inlet-valve guides; or late ignition timing.

Do not attempt to reduce fuel consumption by fitting a smaller size main jet to one or both carburettors (where two are fitted). The size of a main jet has no effect except when the motor-cycle is being ridden with the throttle more than half open. Where the reason for a high fuel consumption is found difficult or impossible to detect, try lowering the tapered jet-needle attached to the throttle valve *one notch*. See that the jet-needle clip beds home properly in the needle groove.

## CARBURETTOR MAINTENANCE

**To Dismantle "Monobloc" Type Carburettor.** First check that the petrol tap is closed and disconnect the petrol pipe from the tank and float-chamber union. Referring to Fig. 3, remove both nuts which secure the carburettor flange to the inlet manifold and unscrew the knurled lock-ring (*2*) on top of the mixing chamber (*3*). Then withdraw the carburettor. While removing it pull the air valve (*17*) and the throttle valve (*5*) from the mixing chamber and tie them up out of the way temporarily. Unless it is desired to inspect these slides closely it is not necessary to remove them from their control cables. Check that the carburettor flange heat-resisting washer is in good condition.

Further dismantling of the carburettor for cleaning and inspection is straightforward. Again referring to Fig. 3, to remove the tapered jet needle (*6*), withdraw the jet-needle clip (*4*) on top of the throttle valve (*5*) and remove the needle. To obtain access to the hinged float (*27*) remove the three screws (*28*) securing the float-chamber cover (*38*) to the float chamber (*37*). Lift out the hinged float (*27*) and withdraw the moulded-nylon needle (*26*). Lay both aside for cleaning. To remove the nylon filter (*see* Fig. 4) unscrew the banjo bolt (*22*), remove the steel washer, the banjo (*23*), and then the nylon filter (*24*).

To remove the main jet (*13*), remove the main-jet cover nut (*12*) and unscrew the jet from the main-jet holder (*14*). Remove the jet block

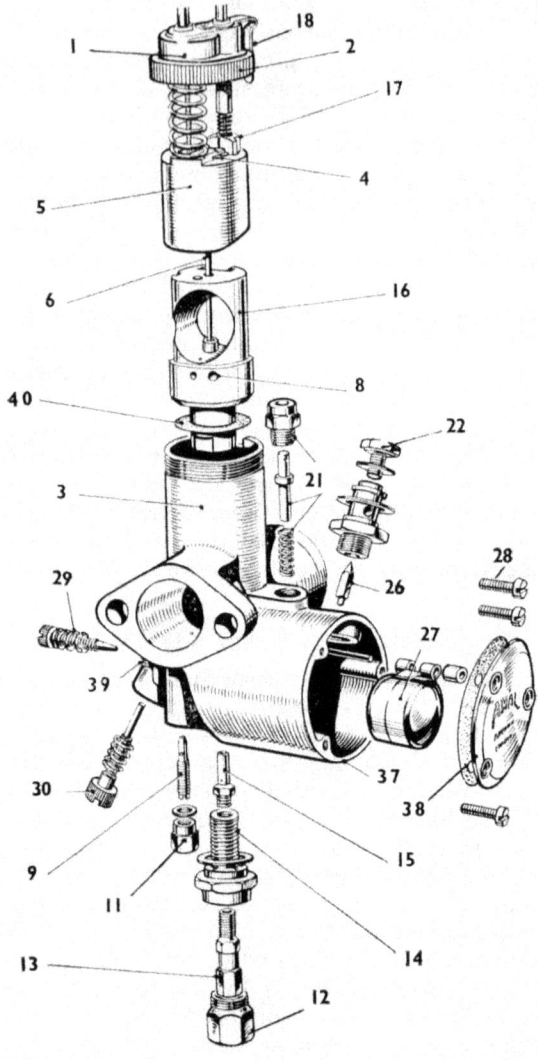

Fig. 3. Exploded View of Amal "Monobloc" Type Carburettor Fitted to all 1955 and Later Norton "Dominator" Models

A key to the numbered parts in Figs. 3, 4 is given on page 8.

(*By courtesy of B.S.A. Motor Cycles Ltd.*)

locating-screw (*39*). Then push or tap out the jet block (*16*) through the larger end of the mixing-chamber body. To remove the pilot jet (*9*) remove the pilot-jet cover nut (*11*) and unscrew the jet.

**Cleaning the Carburettor (1955-65).** Wash all the carburettor components thoroughly clean with petrol and blow air through the various ducts and passages to ensure that they are quite clear. Do not use a fluffy rag for drying purposes. Pay special attention to the small pilot-jet passages in the jet block. Be sure to remove all impurities from the float chamber. Clean the detachable pilot jet (*9*) and also the nylon filter shown at (*24*) in Fig. 4.

**Inspecting Amal Components.** If your carburettor has been in continuous service for a considerable period inspect its various components after dismantling it. Note the following:

1. *The Float Chamber.* Examine it carefully. See that its vent hole is unobstructed and that the float is in perfect condition.

Clean the moulded-nylon needle very thoroughly, and be careful not to damage it. If it tends to stick in its seating, relieve its three bearing edges with a *fine* file. The needle seating shown at (*25*) in Fig. 4 must be absolutely clean. See that the small nylon filter (*24*) is undamaged, and contains no obstructions. Check that the joint faces of the float-chamber cover and the float chamber are not damaged or bruised, and that the joint washer is in sound condition, otherwise some petrol leakage may occur at the cover joint.

2. *The Throttle Valve.* Check that the throttle valve slides up and down in the mixing chamber without excessive play. If excessive play exists, renew the throttle valve. On a model with twin carburettors it is particularly important that *both* throttle valves are in good condition.

3. *The Jet-needle Clip.* The spring clip which secures the tapered jet-needle to the throttle valve must grip the needle firmly. Free rotation of the needle must not occur, otherwise the needle groove will become worn and necessitate a new needle being fitted. When the carburettor is re-assembled be careful to replace the jet-needle with the spring clip in the correct groove (*see* page 8).

4. *The Needle-jet.* Inspect its orifice for signs of wear which are generally present after covering about 15,000 miles. The tapered jet-needle is made of hard stainless-steel and its tapered portion does not wear.

5. *The Jet Block.* Before tapping this home in the mixing chamber verify by blowing that the pilot-jet ducts are unobstructed. Make sure that the jet block fibre-seal is in good condition and renew it if necessary.

6. *The Carburettor Flange.* Examine this for truth with a straight-edge. After a considerable mileage slight distortion sometimes is present, and this can cause an air leak. On a model with twin carburettors examine

the flanges of both carburettors. See that the heat-resisting washer is in sound condition. If it is not, renew it. If the face of a carburettor flange is slightly concave, file the face carefully and then rub the face on emery cloth, laid on a surface plate, until a straight-edge proves the surface to be dead flat. Alternatively have the flange-face ground dead flat.

**To Re-assemble "Monobloc" Type Carburettor.** Assemble the carburettor fitted to 1955 and later models in the reverse order of dismantling. Referring to Fig. 3, screw home the pilot jet (*9*) and the pilot-jet cover nut (*11*), not omitting to replace its washer. Push or tap home the jet block (*16*) and fibre seal (*40*) through the larger end of the mixing chamber (*3*). Check that the fibre seal fitted to the stub of the jet block

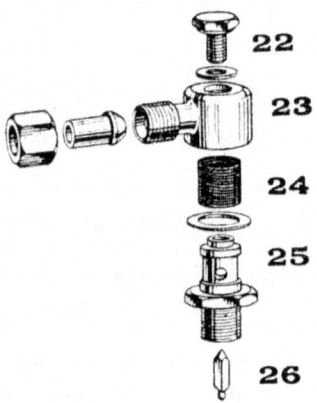

FIG. 4. SHOWING THE NYLON FILTER AND ADJACENT PARTS ON THE AMAL "MONOBLOC" TYPE CARBURETTOR

(*By courtesy of* The Enfield Cycle Co. Ltd.)

is in sound condition. Fit a new seal if necessary. Then fit the jet-block locating screw (*39*). Screw the main-jet holder (*14*) into the jet block after checking that the washer for the holder is sound and that the needle-jet (*15*) is screwed firmly into the top of the main-jet holder. Replace the main-jet cover nut (*11*).

Replace the moulded-nylon needle (*26*) in the float chamber (*37*) and fit the hinged float (*27*) with the *narrow* side of the hinge uppermost. It must contact the nylon needle. Do not omit the short distance collar on the spindle. Afterwards fit the float-chamber cover (*38*) and replace its three securing screws (*28*). Be careful to tighten these three screws evenly. Before replacing the cover it is advisable to renew the washer. Make sure that the float-chamber cover and cover joint-faces are absolutely clean.

Replace items (22)–(24) shown in Fig. 4. Note that the small nylon filter (24) has longitudinal supports moulded to its sides. When replacing the filter see that these supports do not obstruct the feed holes in (25), otherwise some petrol starvation may result. Tighten the banjo bolt (22) securely when the petrol pipe is later connected to the banjo by the union nut.

If previously removed, attach the tapered-jet needle (6) to the throttle valve (5) and secure it with the jet-needle clip (4). Make sure that the clip enters the correct groove on the needle (*see* page 8).

Fit the heat-resisting washer to the face of the inlet manifold. Renew it unless perfect. Some carburettor flanges have a rubber "O" ring. Then smear a little oil on the outside of the throttle valve (5) and ease it and the air valve (17) down into the mixing chamber (3). When easing the throttle valve home, make sure that the tapered jet-needle (6) really enters the hole in the jet block (16).

Offer up the carburettor and secure its flange firmly to the inlet manifold face (to the cylinder head spacer on a 1962 model with down-draught cylinder head) and washer by means of the two nuts. It is very important to tighten these nuts evenly. Tighten down firmly the mixing-chamber knurled lock-ring (2) so as to secure the mixing-chamber cap (1), and see that the throttle valve slides up and down freely when the cap is secured. Finally re-connect the petrol pipe to the tank and float-chamber unions. Tighten the union nuts and the banjo bolt shown at (22) in Fig. 4.

**Throttle Twist-grip Adjustment.** It is desirable always to have the twist-grip adjusted so that there is some *slight stiffness*. This prevents the throttle closing when the hand is removed for signalling, etc. An adjuster screw and lock-nut are provided. Loosen the lock-nut and screw the adjuster in or out as required; afterwards firmly tighten the lock-nut.

# 3 Norton lubrication

A dry-sump (D.S.) lubrication system is included on all 1955 and later Norton O.H.V. vertical-twin engines. This chapter contains full instructions for the correct lubrication of your "Dominator" engine, the gearbox, and the various motor-cycle parts (including components of the electrical system). Not much or frequent attention is necessary, but regular and correct lubrication is *vital* to maintain efficiency and trouble-free running.

## ENGINE LUBRICATION

**The "Dominator" Dry-sump System.** The D.S. lubrication system provided is practically identical on all 1955–65 Norton Twins. The following is an outline of the system.

Engine oil is gravity fed, assisted by suction, from the oil tank through a cylindrical gauze-filter and oil feed-pipe (*see* Fig. 39) to a very efficient Norton gear-type oil pump of the type shown in Fig. 5. This pump is worm-driven inside the timing case and is secured by two nuts. A synthetic-rubber oil-sealing washer under compression forms an oil-tight joint between the oil pump and timing-case cover. An important feature of the oil pump is that the two gears on its return side are twice as wide as the two gears on the feed side. They therefore have double the pumping capacity of the latter and keep the crankcase sump "dry." Hence the term dry-sump or D.S. lubrication.

The feed side of the oil pump forces engine oil through drilled oil-ways in the timing cover to the hollow mainshaft of the off-side flywheel; an extension of this shaft rotates in a timing-cover oil seal. The oil is then pressure-fed through the drilled crankshaft to the two plain big-end bearings of the connecting-rods. Oil splashed from the big-end bearings and flywheels lubricates the two cylinder bores and pistons.

Surplus oil escaping from a non-adjustable oil-pressure release valve (*see* Figs. 6, 7) in the rear of the timing cover builds up to a pre-determined level in the timing case and after lubricating the timing gears and chains drains into the crankcase sump through a drilled hole. The oil-pressure release valve is pre-set to "blow off" if the oil pressure exceeds about 45 lb per sq in. A tiny breather functioning at the inner end of the camshaft regulates the air pressure existing within the crankcase. Surplus oil vapour escaping helps to lubricate the secondary chain (1962 on).

An external pipe connected near the oil tank, to the oil-return pipe (*see* Fig. 39) conveys oil to the hollow O.H.V. rocker spindles, push-rod ends, and valve guides. Surplus oil from the overhead valve-gear drains into the crankcase sump through a hole drilled in the rear of the cylinder block on the off-side.

All surplus oil which drains back into the crankcase sump is sucked up by the return side of the gear-type oil pump and forced back into the oil

FIG. 5. DISMANTLED GEAR-TYPE OIL PUMP FITTED TO ALL 1955 AND LATER "DOMINATOR" MODELS

Observe that the gears on the return side of the pump are twice as wide as those on the feed side to ensure "dry sump" lubrication. For the position of the pump in the engine *see* page 14.

tank through the oil-return pipe. Filters included in the lubrication system are dealt with on page 17.

**Six Essential Points to Remember.** If you respect your "Dominator" engine the following six points are essential to its correct lubrication:
 1. Always replenish the oil tank to the correct level with suitable engine oil of the correct grade.
 2. Run-in a new or a rebored engine for 1,000 miles with great care. Do not get impatient.
 3. Frequently check that the engine oil is circulating properly.
 4. Keep sufficient engine oil in circulation by regularly topping-up the oil tank.
 5. See that the engine oil is clean by changing it regularly.
 6. Clean the filters in the oil tank and crankcase sump at regular intervals.

**Suitable Engine Oils.** Never run on an inferior brand of engine oil or a good oil of unsuitable grade. To obtain maximum performance and minimum wear, replenish the oil tank with one of the following six oils recommended by Norton Motors Ltd.:

 1. Castrol Grand Prix (summer) or XL (winter).
 2. Shell X-100 Motor Oil 50 (summer) or X-100 30 (winter).
 3. Mobiloil D, SAE 50 (summer) or Arctic, SAE 20 (winter).

4. B.P. Energol SAE 50 (summer) or SAE 30 (winter).
5. Regent Havoline 50 (summer) or Havoline 30 (winter).
6. Essolube 50 (summer) or Essolube 30 (winter).

**Running-in.** Careful running-in for the first 1,000 miles is dealt with on page 4.

**To Check Oil Circulation (All 1955–65 Models).** An oil pressure-gauge is not fitted to any models dated later than 1953 and to check that the engine oil is circulating properly it is necessary to remove the oil-tank filler cap and observe whether with the engine running an intermittent stream of oil flows from the orifice of the oil-return pipe. The surface of the oil in the tank should be covered with bubbles. Make a habit of checking the oil circulation before starting out on a run. If the engine has just been started after remaining idle for some time, it is normal for an increased flow of oil from the return-pipe orifice to occur for some minutes. Where no oil flow occurs or it is very irregular, this may be because either the level of oil in the tank is too low or there is leakage at the oil seal between the timing cover and the gear-type oil pump. Leakage may also exist at the oil seal on the end of the off-side flywheel mainshaft. The remedy in both cases is to renew the oil seals after removing the timing-cover. Another possible cause of reduced or irregular oil pressure is a stuck oil-pressure release valve or a broken release-valve spring.

**A Useful Tip.** Occasionally place a finger over the orifice of the oil-return pipe when the engine is ticking-over. This causes more oil to be forced up to the overhead valve-mechanism and flushes out the small holes which feed engine oil to the ball ends of the overhead rockers. Partial obstructions can thereby be cleared.

**Inspect Oil Level in Tank Every 200 Miles.** Before doing this always run the engine for a few minutes after starting up. This is necessary to prevent over filling when topping-up. When the engine is left stationary for some time a considerable amount of oil drains through the oil pump into the crankcase sump and is not returned to the tank by the pump immediately.

On some 1955 models the words *Minimum oil level* are painted on the oil tank, and the oil tank should be kept not less than half full and not more than three-quarters full. If the oil level is above the three-quarters mark the oil pressure builds up in the tank and some oil may be forced through the breather pipe on to the tyres and road.

On all later models always keep the oil level at or near the words *Recommended Oil Level*, usually indicated by a transfer on the outside of the oil tank. Should you allow the oil level to become higher, surplus oil may be discharged through the tank breather-pipe, especially when riding fast, and cause excessive oiling of the secondary chain. Some oil may also get on to the tyres. Too low an oil level in the tank can cause overheating of the engine because of the small amount of oil in circulation. To ensure adequate lubrication of the secondary chain a slightly higher level of oil in the tank is desirable for slow town riding than for hard riding on the open road.

**Lubrication of Overhead Valve-gear.** On all Nortons having O.H.V. vertical-twin engines the overhead valve-gear is automatically lubricated by an external oil-feed pipe connected near the oil tank to the oil-return pipe between the oil pump and tank. Because the overhead valve-gear is at a higher level than the orifice of the oil-return pipe it is necessary for the end of the return pipe to have a restriction. This creates sufficient pressure to force oil to a higher level.

On different oil tanks the restriction at the end of the oil-return pipe varies. Should the valve guides and the overhead rockers appear to receive insufficient lubrication, it is advisable to increase the oil supply by removing the existing oil-pipe union adapter and replacing it with an adapter (Part No. 22148) which has a restriction built into its outlet at the tank end.

**Drain and Refill Oil Tank Every 2,000 Miles.** Drain and refill the oil tank to the correct level with suitable engine oil (*see* page 15) on a new or reconditioned engine after covering 500 miles, again at 1,000 miles, and subsequently at 2,000 mile intervals. On all except some 1955 models the drain plug is located as shown at 2 in Fig. 39. It is advisable to drain the oil tank when the oil is warm. Use a suitable receptacle to catch the oil as it issues from the tank. Remove and wash out the oil tank with petrol or paraffin about every 4,000 miles. When replacing the drain plug be sure to fit the washer and to tighten the plug securely.

**The Oil Tank Filter.** On 1955 models without "featherbed" frames the gauze filter can be very readily removed and it is advisable to disconnect the oil-feed pipe, remove the filter, and clean the filter thoroughly in petrol each time the engine oil is changed, i.e. every 2,000 miles.

On 1956 and later models with a rubber or plastic feed-pipe union it is advisable not to disturb the filter joint. Remove the oil tank from the motor-cycle, complete with filter, every second oil change (i.e. every 4,000 miles) and wash out the tank thoroughly with petrol or paraffin. The filter will then automatically be cleaned without disturbing its joint. Should it be necessary to remove the filter, remove the rubber- or plastic-pipe union, using a ring spanner.

**The Crankcase Filter.** Remove the large corrugated-gauze filter from the crankcase sump each time you change the engine oil (i.e. every 2,000 miles). When the combined filter and drain plug is removed about half a pint of engine oil flows out. Therefore place a suitable receptacle beneath the sump before removing the bronze body of the combined unit by unscrewing its hexagon. This is located at the lowest part of the crankcase sump.

Detach the corrugated-gauze filter by removing the aluminium washer or plate (earlier models) and the wire circlip which secures the filter to the filter body. Be careful not to distort the circlip when removing it. Wash the corrugated-gauze filter and the filter and drain-plug body very thoroughly with petrol and remove any metal particles which may have adhered to them. When re-assembling the combined drain plug and filter make quite sure that the wire circlip beds home snugly in the recess provided. Replace the assembled unit (with washer) and tighten its hexagon firmly.

**The Oil-pressure Release Valve and Filter.** It is extremely unlikely that the valve and filter will need cleaning except during a major engine overhaul after covering a very big mileage. If, however, the oil tank becomes damaged for some reason or the engine oil gets seriously contaminated through neglect to change the oil regularly, it is advisable to remove the pressure-release valve and its filter for thorough cleaning and inspection. No adjustment is necessary.

On 1955-7 "Dominator" engines a small disc-type gauze filter is secured by or soldered to the horizontal oil-pressure release valve body (*see* Fig. 6) which must be removed from the rear of the timing-cover to obtain access to the valve and filter. Before unscrewing and removing the body from the assembled unit, remove the external dome-shaped nut from the rear of the timing-cover. Also withdraw the spring and the oil-pressure release valve plunger.

On all 1958-61 engines and on later models without a boss on the timing-cover for a rev-meter gearbox a cylindrical gauze pressure-release valve is used (*see* Fig. 7). To withdraw the cylindrical gauze-filter and its attached spring, it is only necessary to remove the large hexagon plug and washer from the rear of the timing-cover. To remove the oil-pressure valve itself it is, of course, necessary to remove the timing-cover.

The 1962-5 Special Sports (SS) models have a combined valve and filter unit. It is of the type explained in the caption beneath Fig. 7 and can readily be withdrawn after removing the cap nut from the rear of the timing-cover.

Note that the filter shown in Fig. 7 is the most likely type to become contaminated because of the considerable space surrounding the gauze cartridge. Sludge and carbon deposits tend to accumulate there.

**The Oil Pump Seal.** A conical-shaped oil seal (of oil- and heat-resisting material) surrounds the metal nipple which is a press-fit in the oil-pump body. With the oil pump and timing cover in position, the oil seal must exert light pressure against the conical-shaped seating in the timing cover. In the event of a serious oil failure (rare), not involving the oil pump, occuring suspect a damaged oil seal or one which does not exert slight outward pressure against the seating in the timing cover.

To check whether the oil pump seal is at fault, remove the timing cover and then hold it in its normal position. The oil seal should push the cover

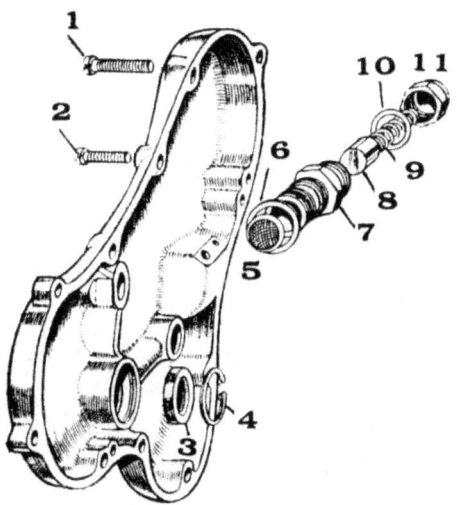

FIG. 6. SHOWING TIMING-COVER AND DETAILS OF OIL-PRESSURE RELEASE VALVE AND FILTER ON 1955–7 ENGINES

1. Long timing-cover screw (six).
2. Short timing-cover screw (six).
3. Oil seal for timing-side mainshaft.
4. Circlip for securing 3.
5. Disc-type gauze filter.
6. Washer for 7.
7. Pressure-release valve body.
8. Plunger.
9. Spring.
10. Washer for 11.
11. Domed hexagon-nut.

away from the crankcase to the extent of 0·010 in. If the oil seal does not exert sufficient pressure, or no pressure, renew it. Alternatively fit several shims between the oil-pump body and the oil seal. Appropriate shims are obtainable from Norton Motors Ltd. or from Norton spares stockists.

**The Timing-cover Oil Seal.** Another rare but possible cause of a serious failure in the lubrication system, not involving the oil pump, is a badly damaged or worn timing-cover oil seal. An unsatisfactory oil seal should be renewed immediately.

A few words about the oil seal will not be amiss. Engine oil is delivered under pressure from the feed side of the oil pump and after passing through the metal nipple surrounded by the conical-shaped oil seal (referred to on page 14) passes through a drilled passage to the timing cover. It emerges into a cavity in the timing-cover. At the exit of this cavity the oil seal is fitted. It engages the plain portion of the timing-side mainshaft and should be closely examined when the timing cover is removed.

**The Crankcase Breather.** A rotary-type breather valve is positioned in the tunnel for the camshaft, in the driving side of the crankcase. It allows

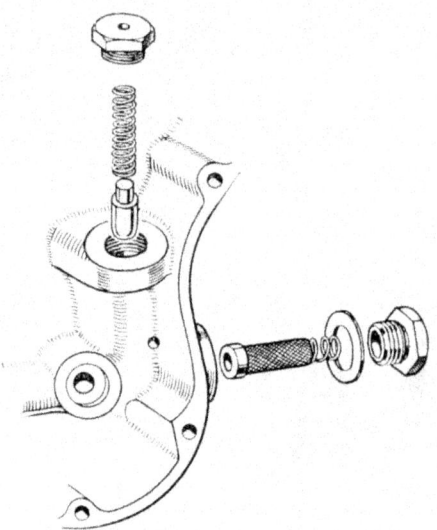

FIG. 7. EXPLODED VIEW OF OIL-PRESSURE RELEASE VALVE AND FILTER ON 1958–61 ENGINES

On the 1962–5 Sports Special (SS) models and machines having a boss on the timing cover for a rev-meter gearbox a larger oil-pressure release valve with a fine-mesh gauze filter on its inner end is fitted. This unit is positioned as shown in Fig. 6 and secured to the timing-case cover by a cap nut.

positive pressure accumulating in the crankcase during the downward piston strokes to escape in the form of oil mist to the oil tank via a rubber hose. On engines numbered 103749 onwards the valve comprises: a stationary plate (below the camshaft bush) retained by a peg; a rotary plate operated by the camshaft; and a spring to keep the rotary plate in contact with the stationary plate.

The correct assembly order for the crankcase breather-valve, which is timed and ported, is to insert the rotary plate face downwards, then the spring, and finally the camshaft. The rotary plate must be absolutely flat. If it is not, renew it. The timing of the valve is affected by wear of the driving dogs. If these become worn, fit a new rotary plate.

When the crankcase is split for bearing renewal it is desirable in the case of early Models 88, 99 and 650 cc Nortons having engines numbered below 103749 to have the later rotary-type crankcase breather-valve fitted to the end of the camshaft. This results in reduced crankcase pressure and discharge of oil mist.

### DYNAMOS, MAGNETOS AND DISTRIBUTOR UNITS

**Dynamo and Magneto Bearings.** The bearings on both types of Lucas instruments are packed with sufficient grease during their initial assembly

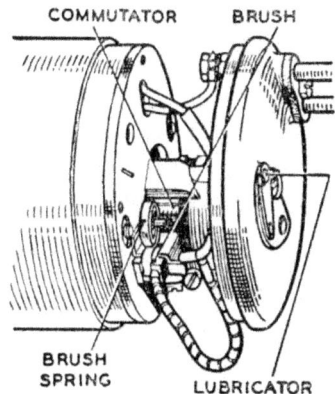

FIG. 8. SHOWING LUBRICATOR ON COMMUTATOR END-BRACKET OF LUCAS E3H DYNAMO (1955 MODELS)

The dynamo cover band is shown removed.

to last for many thousands of miles. Repacking the bearings with grease is not necessary until the instrument require a complete overhaul.

**The Dynamo Commutator.** On 1955 models equipped with magneto ignition, and a Lucas E3H dynamo for charging the battery for lighting purposes, a lubricator (*see* Fig. 8) is provided on the end-bracket of the dynamo commutator. Every 1,000 miles push aside the spring cover and insert a few drops of high quality thin machine-oil through the lubricator. On 1956–7 Norton Twins with magneto ignition and dynamo lighting the commutator of the Lucas E3L dynamo requires no lubrication.

**The Rotating-armature Magneto (1955–65 Models).** On all 1955–65 models not provided with coil ignition a Lucas type K2F or (on SS models) K2FC magneto of the rotating-armature type is fitted. Both types of magneto are similar, but the later type has a contact adjustment different to that provided on the earlier type. The automatic timing-control is enclosed in the timing case and is automatically lubricated, but the cam ring, rocker-arm pivot and the spring of the contact-breaker should be lubricated every 3,000 miles.

The cam ring is fed with lubricant from a felt strip (*see* Fig. 9) contained in a recess in its housing. Oil reaches the surface of the cam ring on which the contact-breaker lever moves from a small circular wick which passes through the thickness of the cam ring.

Remove the contact-breaker cover. Then unscrew and remove the hexagon-headed securing screw and carefully withdraw the contact-breaker from the tapered end of the armature spindle. When the securing

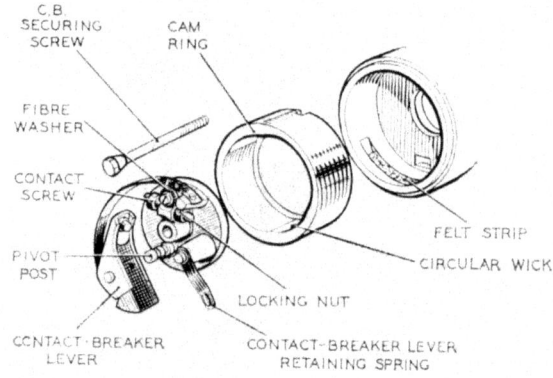

Fig. 9. Contact-Breaker, Cam Ring and Cam-Ring Housing of the Lucas Type K2F, K2FC Magnetos Fitted to 1955–65 Nortons not Provided with Coil Ignition

On the later type K2F, K2FC magnetos fitted to many models the contact-breaker is different (*see* Fig. 10).

screw is completely clear of the threads in the spindle use it to "break" the spindle taper by levering it sideways with the fingers. The contact-breaker will then come away with its securing screw.

Withdraw the cam ring which is a sliding fit in the contact-breaker housing. Clean the inner and outer surfaces of the cam ring and lightly smear them with some Mobilgrease No. 2. Add a few drops of thin machine-oil to the circular wick and the felt strip.

Remove the contact-breaker lever (the rocker arm) and smear its pivot post with a little Mobilgrease No. 2. Use sufficient grease to fill the annular groove. To remove the contact-breaker lever from the pivot post of a contact-breaker fitted to later type magnetos it is necessary to remove the push-on retaining ring (*see* Fig. 10). Do not use this ring again but fit a new one. An alternative method of lubricating the pivot post is to apply a spot of clean engine oil to the tip of the post. By using this method it is not necessary to remove the contact-breaker lever, but you must be careful not to allow any oil to get on or near the contacts.

If you remove the contact-breaker lever on a later type magneto do not lose the fibre washers (*see* Fig. 10) positioned below the lever to ensure true vertical alignment of the fixed and moving contacts. To remove the contact-breaker spring detach the spring from the support on the contact-breaker base. It is secured by a single screw. A small buffer spring is also

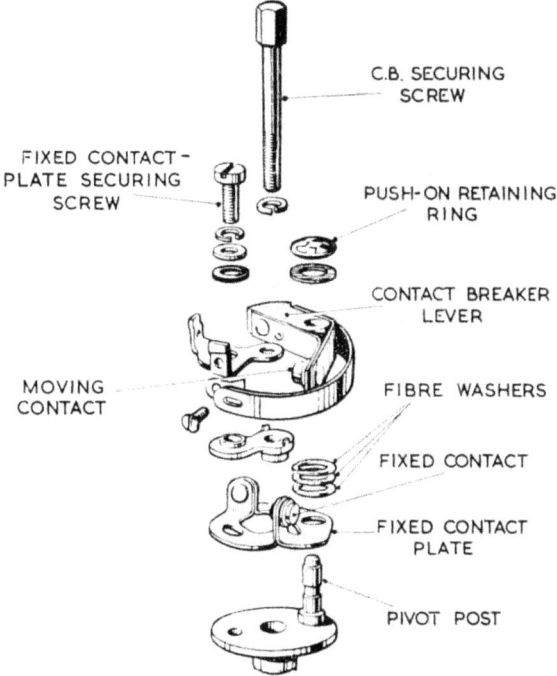

FIG. 10. THE LATER TYPE CONTACT-BREAKER FITTED TO LUCAS K2F, K2FC MAGNETOS SHOWN DISMANTLED
The earlier type contract-breaker is shown in Fig. 9.

provided and must be fitted with its bent portion towards the centre. Earlier type magnetos have no push-on retaining ring for the contact-breaker lever, and to remove the lever from its pivot post swing aside the retaining spring shown in Fig. 9. The previous remarks concerning the contact-breaker spring and buffer spring apply. Check both contacts for condition (*see* page 55).

Reassemble in the reverse order. First replace the cam ring. Lightly smear the contact-breaker spring with some clean engine oil. Fit the contact-breaker lever to the pivot post of the contact-breaker. If an earthing brush is fitted to the back of the base plate, check that it is clean and can move freely before inserting the contact-breaker in the cam ring. When securing the contact-breaker assembly to the armature spindle make sure that the projecting key on the tapered portion of the contact-breaker base plate properly engages the key-way of the spindle. See that the spring does not contact the cam ring. Do not over-tighten the contact-breaker securing screw. Finally check and if necessary adjust the contact-breaker gap (*see* page 64).

**The Contact-breaker and Distributor Unit (1958–63 Coil Ignition Models).** With the exception of 1962–5 Special Sports (SS) models all 1958 and later "Dominator" Nortons have coil ignition. A contact-breaker and distributor unit (*see* Fig. 37) is horizontally mounted behind the cylinder block and is chain-driven from the intermediate timing gear. Every 6,000 miles lubricate the automatic ignition-advance mechanism with clean engine oil. Similarly lubricate the cam and pivot post for the contact-breaker lever. The cleaning and lubrication of the contact-breaker and distributor unit should be done as a combined operation. Detailed instructions are given on page 53.

## THE MOTOR-CYCLE PARTS

**Top-up Gearbox Every 1,000 Miles.** All 1955 and some 1956 Nortons have a Burman gearbox, but all later models have an A.M.C. gearbox. For lubricating both types of gearbox use the *summer grade* engine oils recommended on page 15. Topping-up both types of gearbox in the same manner.

Referring to Fig. 39 remove the circular or oval plate (6) secured by two small screws to the gearbox cover. Also unscrew and remove the gearbox oil-level plug (8) which is located close to the kick-starter spindle. Then, using a funnel, pour in summer grade engine oil through the orifice exposed by removal of the plate until oil begins to trickle from the oil-level plug hole. When replenishing the gearbox allow ample time for the oil to find its natural level. Rotating the gears with the kick-starter will assist replenishment. Finally replace the oil-level plug and the plate, tightening both down securely. Do not forget to replace their washers.

**Change the Gearbox Oil Every 5,000 Miles.** After covering 500 miles with a new or re-conditioned gearbox, and subsequently every 5,000 miles, drain the gearbox and refill it with fresh *summer grade* engine oil (*see* page 15). The screwed drain-plug is located low down at the rear of the gearbox casing. Before filling the gearbox make sure that you replace the drain plug and its washer. Tighten the drain plug securely.

**Primary Chain Lubrication.** To keep the primary chain in good condition and to avoid the necessity for frequently adjusting it for tension, top-up the oil-bath chain case after covering 500 miles; then regularly every 1,000 miles. Use Wakefield's "Castrolite," Shell X-100 20, Price's Energol SAE 20, Essolube 20, Regent Havoline 20, or Mobiloil Arctic.

Remove the inspection cover after swinging aside its securing spring and also remove the oil-level plug from the outer portion of the chain case.

Fig. 11. Showing Oil-Bath Chain Case Enclosing the Primary Chain and Clutch, and on 1958–65 Models the Alternator also

Illustrations of the oil-bath chain case with outer cover removed, fitted to 1955–7 and 1958–65 models, are included on pages 95 and 96 respectively.

1. Quickly-detachable inspection cover.  2. Oil-level plug.
3. Nut securing near-side footrest and chain-case cover.

With the motor-cycle upright then pour in oil through the inspection-cover hole until it begins to drip from the oil-level plug hole. Afterwards replace the oil-level plug (with washer) and the inspection cover. Every 8,000 miles drain and refill the oil-bath chain case. Draining necessitates removing the outer portion of the case (*see* page 95). Look for damaged rollers. These can damage an alternator where present.

**Lubricating Secondary Chain.** On all 1955–65 models the secondary chain is automatically lubricated by a pipe from the oil-tank vent. Oil vapour is fed from the vent pipe to the forward end of the chain guard or chain case (where fitted). The amount of oil vapour fed to the secondary chain by the tank vent pipe varies according to how the motor-cycle is ridden. When using it just for riding to work the chain may not receive much oil, but when speeding on motorways it may receive excessive oil.

The safest method of ensuring sufficient lubrication of the secondary chain on all models is to watch the chain and lubricate it whenever it runs dry. It is usually sufficient to do this about every 1,000 miles, but more often on some machines, especially earlier models. To do this brush grease on to the chain while rotating the rear wheel by hand. Suitable greases are Castrolease Grease Graphited, Mobilgrease No. 2, Energrease A.O., Esso Fluid Grease and Regent Marfak No. 2.

Engine oil (*see* page 15) can, of course, be used for lubricating the secondary chain and in this case the best method is to rotate the rear wheel by hand while applying an oil-can to the lower run of the chain. See that the oil falls on the bearing surfaces and not merely on the rollers. Sufficient chain lubrication is important.

About every 3,500–4,000 miles, where the chain is not fully enclosed by a chain case, remove the chain and clean it thoroughly by submerging it in paraffin. If the chain is allowed to soak thoroughly, all the dirt will be extracted. Hang the chain up to dry and, before replacing it, immerse it for at least ten minutes in a receptacle containing a quantity of *warm* chain lubricant (*see* above). This will penetrate to all its bearing surfaces. Alternatively allow the chain to soak for several hours in engine oil (*see* page 15).

**Increasing Oil Vapour Feed to Secondary Chain.** On Norton Twins a rubber extension of the crankcase-breather pipe diverts oil vapour to the ground at a point near the centre-stand pivot. The extension can be removed by taking out the single screw which secures it to the back of the crankcase. The copper pipe can then be partially straightened out and the rubber extension shortened so that it discharges on to the secondary chain where it passes over the gearbox-mainshaft sprocket. By doing this, additional oil vapour is fed to the secondary chain.

**Suitable Greases.** For wheel hub lubrication and the lubrication of all motor-cycle components having grease nipples, use Castrolease Heavy, MP Mobilgrease, Shell Retinax A or C.D., Regent Marfak or B.P. Energrease C3.

Fill the grease-gun adequately and try it out before applying it to grease nipples. Charge the grease-gun with suitable grease so that the grease is on the *top* side of the piston. Special grease canisters are available having loose collars provided with holes. To charge the grease-gun with this type of canister remove its screwed top-cap, place the barrel of the gun over the hole in the central fixing-plate of the canister, and press it down firmly. Afterwards replace the screwed top-cap on the grease-gun. If a grease canister of the type referred to is not available, charge the grease-gun by hand, using a lath or similar implement.

**The Steering Head.** On earlier models (about 1955-6) grease nipples are provided for lubricating the ball bearings, but later Nortons have no grease nipples, the bearings being initially packed with sufficient grease for very many thousands of miles. Where grease nipples are provided, apply the grease-gun every 2,000 miles.

**Recommended Damping Oils for All Front Forks.** The Norton "Roadholder" telescopic-type front forks fitted to all 1955-65 "Dominator" models require to be periodically drained and replenished with fresh damping oil. Suitable damping oils for replenishing *all* 1955-65 front forks are: Wakefield's Castrolite (SAE 20), Mobiloil Arctic (SAE 20), B.P. Energol (SAE 20), Essolube 20 (SAE 20) and Shell X-100 Motor Oil 20/20W (SAE 20). The above oils are recommended by Norton Motors Ltd.

**Replenishing Front Forks (1955-8 Models).** Drain both fork legs and replenish with new damping oil about every 5,000 miles, or whenever the movement of the forks deteriorates. Use the following procedure.

Remove the hexagon-headed filler plug from the top of one fork leg. Also remove the small cheese-headed drain plug (and washer) from the bottom of the fork leg at the rear. Then drain off all the damping oil into a suitable receptacle. Allow several minutes for draining. With the front brake applied, move the telescopic forks up and down so as to expel the last drop of damping oil. Drain the other fork leg similarly and then replace both drain plugs and their washers. Now, with the motor-cycle on its stand, pour into each fork leg, using a small funnel, a measured *quarter of a pint* of fresh damping oil. Afterwards operate the forks several times to eliminate any air-locks which may exist, and finally replace the two filler plugs and their washers.

**To Replenish Front Forks (1959-63 Models).** The 1959-63 "Roadholder" telescopic-type front forks are of somewhat different design to the 1955-8 forks and the damping oil should be drained and renewed about every 10,000 miles, or whenever the normal characteristics of the forks deteriorate. Where new front forks are concerned it is advisable to change the damping oil after covering about 1,000 miles, i.e. at the end of the bedding-in period. Any swarf or metal particles which may have accumulated can then be removed with the damping oil.

Both fork legs have a drain plug comprising a cheese-headed screw located at the bottom of the fork leg at the rear. Place a suitable receptacle beneath one drain plug and remove the plug and its aluminium or fibre washer. Hold the front brake on and move the forks up and down to expel all damping oil. Allow the oil to drain for several minutes and then repeat the draining procedure for the other fork leg. Then replace both drain plugs and their washers, and place the machine on its centre stand.

Unscrew the two large filler plugs from the tops of both fork legs and "pull up" the front wheel to expose the springs. Lay a block of wood or box under the front wheel to hold the springs clear. Then, using two spanners, unscrew the filler-plug nuts from the tops of the damper rods. Remove the wood block or box from beneath the front wheel and allow the telescopic forks to extend fully. Using a suitable small funnel, pour a measured *five fluid ounces* (*142 cc*) of new damping oil into each fork leg. Because of the springs inside the fork-leg main tubes the damping oil is somewhat slow to penetrate downwards and it is necessary to be patient when re-filling the fork legs.

Before replacing the two filler plugs and their washers make quite sure that their lock-nuts are screwed right down to the ends of the threads on the damper rods. Lock the two together and finally tighten the two filler plugs.

**Replenishing Front Forks (1964–5 Models).** The 1964–5 forks are the same except for dimensions to the 1959–63 type. On a new machine the telescopic front forks should be drained and the damping oil renewed after covering about 1,000 miles. Subsequent draining and renewal should be effected about every 10,000 miles or whenever the normal functioning of the telescopic front forks has deteriorated.

The fork springs abut against the filler plugs and therefore before removing these plugs it is essential to take the weight off the front wheel by placing the machine on its central stand. Otherwise the forks are liable to collapse.

With the motor-cycle on its centre stand, unscrew the hexagon-headed filler plugs from the tops of both fork legs. Then place a suitable receptacle to catch oil draining off from the fork leg to be dealt with. Remove the drain plug screw from the bottom of the fork leg at the rear side. Be careful not to lose its small washer. Now drain off all oil. Tilting the front wheel to one side will assist draining. Drain the other fork leg of all damping oil in a similar manner. Complete draining will take an appreciable time. When both fork legs have been fully drained replace the two small drain plugs and their washers, and tighten the drain plugs securely.

Now, using a measured container, pour in *five fluid ounces* (*142 cc*) of new damping oil (*see* page 27) into the top of each fork leg. Afterwards replace the two filler plugs and their washers. Note that the air space between the fork springs and the insides of the tubes is very small and when replenishing the front forks be careful to avoid loss of damping oil by spilling.

**Girling Rear-suspension Units.** All 1955–65 "swinging arm" models have Girling rear-suspension units except some 1956 and 1957 machines which have Armstrong units. These proprietary units are sealed by the makers and do not need any topping-up.

Occasionally clean and grease the external cam-ring adjusters provided on 1957 and later units, but not on some earlier types. These adjusters give three different pre-loadings of the main springs (*see* page 117). Should movement of the telescopic tubes be accompanied by a rubbing or squeaking noise, remove the two half-circlips securing each top-cover and apply some grease to the outside diameter of the spring.

**Armstrong Rear-suspension Units.** These rear-suspension units, fitted to some 1956 and 1957 models, are sealed like the Girling units and need no topping-up or lubrication. The damping oil inserted by the makers will last for an indefinite running period. It is advisable occasionally to grease the external adjusters for giving two different pre-loadings of the main springs (*see* page 117).

**Wheel Hubs (1955–65).** The bearings of all full width light-alloy hubs are packed with grease during initial assembly, and grease nipples are not provided. About every 10,000 miles remove both wheels, dismantle and clean the hubs, and repack the bearings with suitable grease (*see* page 26).

**Brake Lubrication.** Every 2,000 miles inject some grease with a grease-gun through the nipple provided for lubricating the rear-brake pedal shaft. At the same time oil the rear-brake rod joints, the exposed front-brake cable and its "U" clip. Every 5,000 miles grease the brake cams (sparingly), the cam spindles, and the brake-shoe pivot pins.

**The Handlebar Controls.** Apply the oil-can every 1,000 miles to the control cables and levers. Oil all linkage pins and the cable nipples (where fitted). When it is found necessary to fit a new cable, charge its casing with grease, using a length of rubber tube in conjunction with the grease-gun to inject grease.

**The Dipper Switch.** Every 5,000 miles apply some thin machine-oil to the moving parts of the handlebar dipper-switch. Be careful not to apply excessive oil otherwise the switch may be short-circuited.

**Speedometer-drive Gearbox.** Every 2,000 miles apply the grease-gun to the nipple located on top of the speedometer-drive gearbox. This small gearbox is positioned on the off-side of the rear-wheel hub.

**The Saddle Pivot.** On earlier "Dominators" not provided with a dual-seat, every 2,000 miles oil the front pivot for the saddle.

**Stands.** Occasionally oil the pivot bolts of both stands of an earlier model, and the pivot bolt of the centre stand of a later type Norton.

# 4 The lighting system (magneto ignition)

1955–65 Norton "Dominators" with magneto ignition have two types of Lucas 6-volt lighting systems. All 1955–7 models have a Lucas magneto mounted behind the cylinder block and a Lucas E3H or E3L dynamo positioned in front of the cylinder block. A Lucas compensated voltage-control unit at the front of the tool tray under the dualseat controls battery charging by regulating automatically the dynamo output.

All 1962–5 Sports Special (SS) models and the 1964–5 750 cc "Atlas" also have a Lucas magneto mounted behind the cylinder block, but there is no dynamo in front of it. Instead a Lucas type RM19 alternator is provided, its rotor being secured to an extension of the engine near-side mainshaft. Alternator output is controlled automatically, and a Lucas a.c. rectifier converts the a.c. current to d.c. current before it reaches and charges the battery (two batteries on 1964–5 SS models and the "Atlas").

Except on coil-ignition models the lighting system is, of course, entirely independent of the ignition system dealt with in Chapter 6 on pages 87–9.

### DYNAMO MAINTENANCE (1955–7)

**Lubrication.** No lubrication of the dynamo armature-bearings is necessary until the dynamo requires a general overhaul, but a lubricator is provided for the commutator on the Lucas E3H dynamo fitted to 1955 models. This requires occasional lubrication (*see* pages 60–6).

**Lucas Servicing.** You should submit the complete dynamo about every 12,000 miles to a Lucas service depot for dismantling, cleaning, servicing and re-packing of the armature bearings with grease.

**To Prevent Shorting.** Before making any wiring adjustments or removing the lighting switch from the Lucas headlamp or panel (1955–7), always disconnect the lead from the battery *negative terminal*. Where a connector is fitted push back the rubber shield and unscrew the two-piece connector. Be careful to see that the connector half which is not removed does not contact any metal part of the motor-cycle. If this should happen a most serious short would occur and the battery would become badly discharged. It is not necessary to disconnect the lead from the battery negative terminal when merely inspecting the commutator brushes and the commutator itself.

THE LIGHTING SYSTEM (MAGNETO IGNITION) 31

**Inspect Commutator Brushes and Commutator Every 6,000 Miles.** The Lucas E3H dynamo, and the later E3L type, will normally run entirely satisfactorily for many thousands of miles with no attention other than a careful inspection of the commutator brushes and the commutator surface every 6,000 miles. This attention is important. To obtain access to the brushes and commutator, remove the metal cover-band from the commutator end-bracket of a Lucas E3H dynamo, or the end cover from a Lucas E3L dynamo (*see* Figs. 8, 12).

**The Brushes (1955–7).** Both brushes must *move freely* in their box-type holders and make firm and good contact with the surface of the commutator. They must also be absolutely clean.

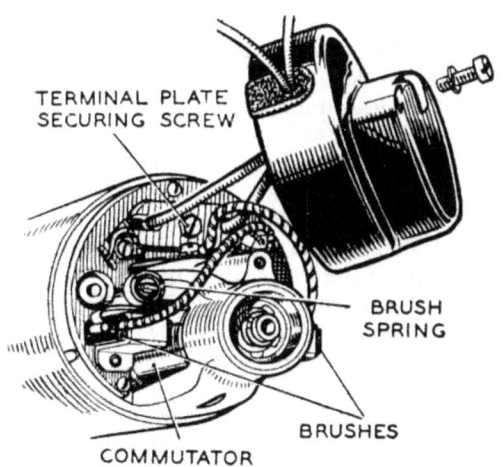

FIG. 12. COMMUTATOR END OF LUCAS E3L DYNAMO WITH COVER REMOVED (1956–7)

The general layout differs from that of the Lucas E3H dynamo fitted to 1955 models and shown in Fig. 8.

To check that each brush slides freely in its holder, hold back the brush retaining-spring and gently pull on its flexible lead, being careful to see that the spring is quite clear of the brush holder. The brush should return to its original position immediately you *gently* release its lead. If a brush sticks in its holder, it is probably dirty and it should be removed and cleaned with a petrol-moistened cloth. *Always replace a brush in its original position.*

Examine both brushes for unevenness and wear. The faces of the brushes in contact with the commutator should be uniformly polished. If after long service the brushes have become worn and shortened to

$\frac{3}{16}$ in. length and do not bed down properly on the commutator, renewal of the brushes is essential. Generally it is wise to renew brushes *before* serious wear occurs, as this prevents sparking which is liable to cause blackening of the commutator segments and unsteady charging of the battery. Genuine Lucas brushes should always be fitted. They require to be carefully bedded to the commutator surface and it is therefore advisable always to have new brushes fitted by a Lucas service agent.

Inspect both brush springs and see that they have ample springiness to keep the brushes firmly pressed against the commutator when the dynamo armature is rotating. Springs having sufficient tension are particularly necessary when the brushes have been in service for a long time and have become considerably worn. Weak springs (fortunately rare) should immediately be renewed.

**The Commutator (1955-57).** Inspect the surface of the commutator segments. It should be clean and free from any trace of oil or dirt; it should also be *dark bronze* in colour and *highly polished* by contact with the carbon brushes. Should oil find its way on to the commutator of a Lucas E3H dynamo through excessive injection of oil into the lubricator shown in Fig. 8, sparking will occur and carbon and copper dust is likely to collect in the grooves between the commutator segments.

The best way to clean a dirty or blackened commutator is to remove from its box-type holder one of the two carbon brushes and, inserting a smooth dry cloth, press it with a suitably-shaped piece of wood firmly against the commutator surface while slowly rotating the engine by hand. Should the commutator be very dirty, moisten the cloth with petrol before inserting it.

**To Remove Dynamo.** On 1955–7 models first disconnect its electrical leads. Then from the timing case remove the three dome nuts provided with a screwdriver slot (1955–6 models), or the three chromium-plated cheese-headed screws (1957 models). Finally release the single screw securing the dynamo clamping strap and withdraw the dynamo.

**Compensated Voltage-control (1955–7).** All 1955–7 Nortons provided with dynamo-lighting equipment have a Lucas C.V.C. unit (*see* Fig. 13) housed at the front end of the tool tray beneath the dualseat.

The unit is connected between dynamo and battery. It comprises a cut-out (an automatic switch) to prevent discharge of the battery when the dynamo is not charging, and a voltage regulator which operates on the trembler principle and regulates dynamo output. The regulator ensures that the battery is automatically kept properly charged by varying the dynamo output according to the state of charge of the battery and the load imposed on it.

In all three lighting switch positions (*see* page 1) the dynamo output is controlled and this relieves you of any responsibility as regards charging the battery. The voltage regulator begins to function when the dynamo voltage reaches about 7·3 volts. During a daylight run with the battery well charged and the lighting switch in the "OFF" position the ammeter needle may indicate a charge of only 1–2 amps because the dynamo gives only a trickle charge. There is consequently no risk of overcharging.

As soon as the lamps are switched on, the voltage regulator increases the dynamo output. Switching the lamps on after a long run with the

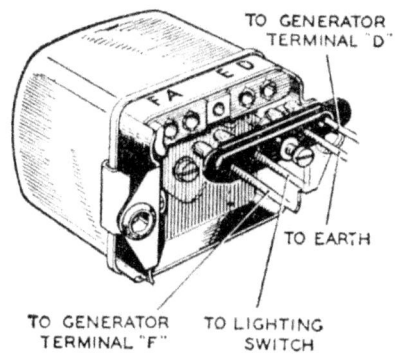

FIG. 13. LUCAS COMPENSATED VOLTAGE-CONTROL UNIT (1955–7)

battery voltage high often causes the ammeter needle to register a temporary discharge, but the voltage falls fairly quickly and the regulator responds, thus causing the dynamo output to balance the lamp load.

**Do Not Interfere with the C.V.C. Unit.** The 1955–7 unit is correctly adjusted and sealed by the makers and should normally be left alone. Trouble rarely develops except when the contacts oxidize or become welded together through accidental crossing of the dynamo field and positive leads. Fig. 13 shows the C.V.C. unit connexions. Keep these connexions tight and the insulation in good condition. If the dynamo functions satisfactorily and the general condition of the battery is good, suspect a faulty C.V.C. unit if persistent overcharging or undercharging of the battery takes place. Get the unit thoroughly checked over at a Lucas service depot.

**No Fuse Is Provided.** The 1955–7 Lucas dynamo-lighting system has no fuse, this being quite unnecessary. There is no risk of excess current damaging the equipment if you keep all wiring connexions clean and tight.

**The Ammeter.** Except on some 1955–7 de Luxe models which have the Lucas ammeter (*see* Fig. 1) fitted on an instrument panel, this is mounted on top of the Lucas headlamp. It is of the centre-zero type and shows at a glance whether the battery is being charged or discharged. As previously mentioned, it normally indicates only a very small charge when the lighting switch is in the "OFF" position, dynamo output then being regulated by the C.V.C. unit.

### THE ALTERNATOR AND RECTIFIER
### (1962–5 SS and 1964–5 "Atlas" Models)

**The Lucas RM19 Alternator.** The alternator (*see* Fig. 14) which comcomprises a stator and a rotor produces a.c. current for passing to the

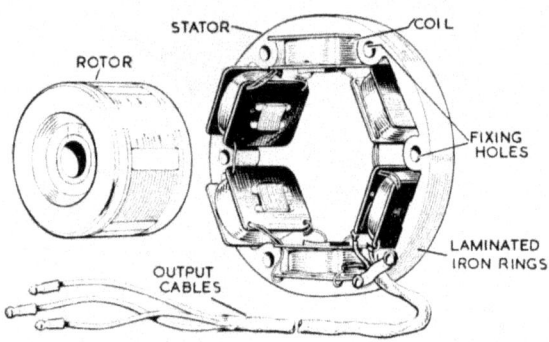

FIG. 14. THE ROTOR AND STATOR OF THE LUCAS RM19 ALTERNATOR

The stator is fixed by three studs projecting from the rear half of the oil-bath chaincase and the rotor is secured to the near-side flywheel mainshaft (*see* Fig. 45). The alternator on 1962–5 magneto-ignition SS models has a stator with a smaller output than on the coil-ignition models. The cable colours are green and white, green and black, and green and yellow.

battery through the rectifier which converts the a.c. current into d.c. current. The alternator, unlike the Lucas E3H or E3L dynamo, has no commutator, commutator brushes, bearings, or oil seals. It thus requires no maintenance other than occasionally checking that its leads are intact and its connexions clean and tight.

When you have to remove the outer portion of the oil-bath chaincase examine the grommet in the rear portion. If it has perished renew it, otherwise the leads may chafe on the rather sharp edge of the hole. Further notes concerning the alternator and the removal of its stator and rotor are given on page 96.

**Increasing Alternator Output (1958 Onwards).** If the battery becomes badly discharged, an increased alternator charging rate can be obtained by making a simple alteration to the wiring as described on page 51.

**The Lucas Rectifier (1958 Onwards).** This device which converts a.c. current to d.c. current and permits the current to flow in one direction only requires no attention other than occasionally to check that its

THE LIGHTING SYSTEM (MAGNETO IGNITION) 35

connexions are clean and tight. Pay special attention to the earth lead connexion and the central bolt. Under no circumstances use a spanner on the clamp nuts which clamp the rectifier plates together. The clamping pressure is very carefully set during initial assembly by the makers so as to provide correct rectifier performance.

A separate nut is provided to attach the selenium type rectifier to the motor-cycle and it is important to periodically check that the rectifier is firmly secured to the underside of the tool-tray (beneath the dualseat) or, on later models beneath the front of the petrol tank or, to the rear side of the battery box. To ensure a good electrical connexion, firm metal-to-metal contact must exist.

### CARE OF THE BATTERY (1955–65 Models)

**Lucas and Exide Batteries.** The 6-volt battery on all except earlier type Norton "Dominators" is well protected, being housed inside the battery box on the near-side of the machine. The Lucas and Exide batteries used are both of the lead-acid type. During 1955 a Lucas PUW-7E-4 or a later PUZ7E/9 battery was fitted, but from 1956 onwards all "Dominators" except de Luxe models and two 1964–5 Sports Specials (Models 88SS, 650SS) and the 1964–5 750 "Atlas") are provided with a Lucas PUZ7E/11 battery.

De Luxe models are equipped with an Exide 3EV9 or 3EV11 battery instead of a Lucas battery. *The Exide and Lucas batteries require similar maintenance.* The 1964–5 Sports Specials and 750 "Atlas" have *two* Lucas 6-volt ultra-lightweight MKZ9E-2 batteries provided, a most unusual feature. These two batteries are connected in series. The maintenance they need is the same as for other Lucas batteries.

On all 1955–7 models the battery is charged by a dynamo, but on all later models by an alternator. When battery renewal, is called for on earlier Nortons, the Lucas PUZ7E/11 battery is strongly recommended.

**Five Important Maintenance Points.** Upon battery condition depend the lamps and horn, and on coil-ignition models the ignition of the fuel also. Regular maintenance of the battery is *vitally* important to keep it at full capacity. It is important to observe these five points:

1. Always keep the battery well charged.
2. Once a fortnight (more often in warm climates) check the level of the electrolyte in the battery cells, and if necessary top-up the cells with *distilled* water.
3. Keep the battery and its terminals clean, and the terminals tight.
4. See that the *earth* lead to the battery is always connected to the *positive* terminal of the battery.
5. If you do not ride your "Dominator" for a considerable time, fully charge the battery, remove it, and have it charged at a garage at fortnightly intervals.

**Charging the Battery (1955-65).** Note the remarks on pages 32 and 50 concerning the lighting switch and battery charging. If the battery becomes under-charged, run as much as possible with the lighting switch in the "OFF" position so that the dynamo or alternator trickle-charges the battery without any current being consumed for lighting.

Lead-acid batteries used in conjunction with alternators, owing to a small leakage occurring at the rectifier, lose their charge slightly more quickly than when used with dynamo-lighting sets. Therefore if you own

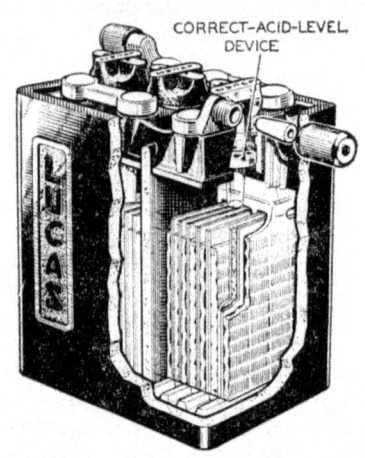

Fig. 15. Cut-away View of Lucas PUZ7E/11 Battery Fitted to Most 1956 and Later Norton Twins

a Norton not provided with a dynamo and do not use it for several days it is a good plan to disconnect the battery *earth* lead to prevent any discharge occurring at the rectifier. When leaving a coil-ignition model standing for an appreciable time with the engine stationary, always be sure to switch off the ignition, because if the contact-breaker contacts happen to be closed some discharge may occur through them.

**Topping-up the Battery Cells (1955-65).** About once a fortnight (more often in warm climates) disconnect the battery leads and its metal securing strap and remove the battery (from the battery box on most models). Then remove the battery lid, clean the top of the battery, and remove the three filler plugs. Examine the level of the electrolyte in each cell after the machine has been left standing, not immediately after a run. When doing this never hold a naked light near the filler-plug holes. The level is correct on Lucas batteries when it is in line with the separator guard, or (on earlier batteries) with the top edges of the plate separators (*see* Fig. 15).

## THE LIGHTING SYSTEM (MAGNETO IGNITION)

The Lucas MKX9E-2 batteries fitted to 1964-5 Sports Specials and the 750 cc "Atlas" have a translucent case and the electrolyte level can be observed without peering through the filler-plug holes. A coloured marker line on the case indicates the correct level. On the Exide 3EV9 and 3EV11 batteries fitted to de Luxe Nortons the electrolyte level should be up to $\frac{1}{8}$ in. above the top of the separators.

If the electrolyte level is below what it should be, add *distilled* water as required to bring the level correct. Topping-up should always be effected *before* a charge run, as the agitation caused while riding, and the "gassing," can be relied upon to thoroughly mix the solution.

If the battery on a dynamo-lighting model needs to be topped-up very often, it is possible that the C.V.C. unit requires adjustment by a Lucas service agent. Should one cell require more frequent topping-up than the others probably the battery case is cracked and battery renewal is called for.

The earlier Lucas PUZ7E/9 and the later type PUZ7E/11 batteries both have an acid-level device (*see* Fig. 15) provided, and this can conveniently be used for topping-up with distilled water. To top-up the cells of a Lucas PUW-7E-4, Lucas MKZ9E-2, or an Exide battery, not provided with an acid-level device, use a Lucas battery filler.

To top-up each battery cell having an acid-level device, pour distilled water round its flange (not down the tube) until no more drains through into the cell. This occurs when the level of the electrolyte reaches the bottom of the central tube and prevents any further escape of air displaced by the water added. Lift the tube slightly to allow the small quantity of water in the flange to drain into the cell; the level of the electrolyte will then be correct.

When using a Lucas battery filler for topping-up, insert its nozzle (*see* Fig. 16) into each cell until the nozzle rests on the separator guard or the top edges of the separators. Hold the battery filler in this position until the air bubbles cease to rise in the glass container. The cell is then topped-up to the correct level.

**Replenishing Lucas Battery Filler.** When replenishing a battery filler see that the screw-on nozzle is replaced correctly. The rubber washer must be fitted over the valve with the small peg in the centre of the valve engaging the hole in the projecting boss of the washer.

**After Topping-up the Battery.** Before replacing each filler plug make sure that its vent hole is clear. A choked vent will result in an increase in pressure in the cell owing to "gassing" and this can result in trouble. Remove any dirt with a bent wire and also wipe the top of the battery thoroughly clean. See that the rubber sealing-washer for each vent plug is in good condition and tighten the three filler plugs firmly. Afterwards replace the battery cover, connect up the battery-terminal leads, and with the metal strap secure the battery in the battery box. Be quite sure to connect the leads to the battery terminals correctly. *On no account connect the earth lead to the battery negative terminal.* On an alternator model even momentary wrong connexion will damage the rectifier.

**The Battery Terminals.** The leads connected to the battery should always make good electrical contact with its positive and negative terminals. Should the battery become out of circuit through faulty

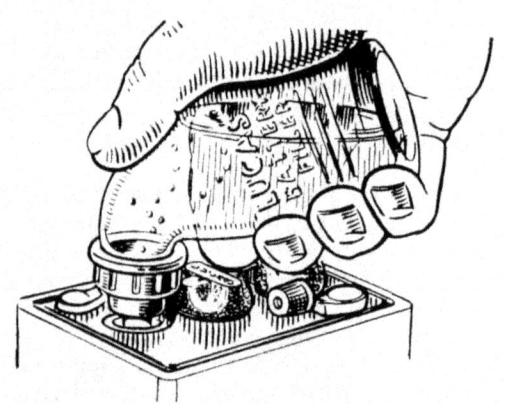

FIG. 16. TOPPING-UP A CELL OF A BATTERY WITH A LUCAS BATTERY FILLER

A battery filler need not be used where the battery has an acid-level device as shown in Fig. 15. Never use tap water for topping-up. Distilled water is obtainable from most garages and chemists.

contact, the lamp bulbs will burn out, even at quite low engine revolutions. Keep the terminals clean and grease them occasionally with vaseline to prevent corrosion. Examine the wire ends periodically to see if they have corroded. On Lucas batteries clean up each terminal and the lead end with a smooth file if you have any doubt about the lead making good and firm electrical contact with the terminal screw. Exide batteries have terminal posts with set-screws which secure the soldered-on tag terminals of the leads. The set-screws must make perfect contact with the terminal posts.

**Connecting Battery Leads.** To connect the leads to a Lucas battery the following is the correct procedure for each lead. Unscrew the knurled plastic terminal-nut and withdraw the collet (a small thick washer). Bare the end of the cable about $\frac{1}{2}$ in. and thread the bared end through the knurled nut and collet. Coil up surplus wire against the end of the collet, and then feed back the collet and wire into the knurled terminal-nut. Screw the nut firmly on to the terminal post, but avoid excessive tightening.

THE LIGHTING SYSTEM (MAGNETO IGNITION)     39

The leads for connecting to an Exide battery have soldered-on tag terminals, and the battery terminals have set-screws. To connect the leads, remove the terminal set-screws, thread on the lead tags, and replace and tighten the set-screws.

**Battery Storage.** A battery when not in use must always be given a refresher charge from a garage charger every 2–3 weeks. Lead-acid batteries when not used, slowly discharge; batteries left standing for long

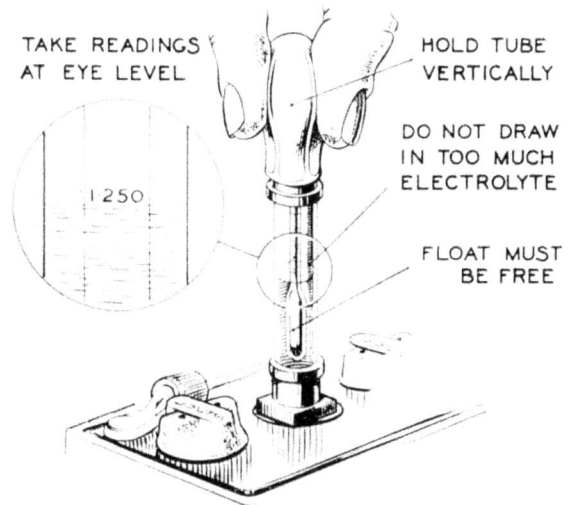

FIG. 17. CHECKING THE SPECIFIC GRAVITY OF THE BATTERY ELECTROLYTE WITH A LUCAS HYDROMETER

This is the most satisfactory way of ascertaining the state of charge of a battery.

periods without being charged deteriorate, their plates becoming sulphated and often permanently spoiled. Do not remove the electrolyte from a battery placed in storage.

**Checking Battery Condition (1955–65).** Occasionally remove the battery and examine its state of charge by taking hydrometer readings (specific gravity values) of the electrolyte in each cell. A hydrometer cannot be used for a Lucas MKZ9E-2 battery. The method of doing this is illustrated in Fig. 17. The Lucas hydrometer shown contains a graduated float which indicates the specific gravity of the electrolyte in the battery cell from which a sample is taken.

When a sample has been taken from a cell and checked it must, of course, be returned to the same cell. The S.G. readings should be approximately *the same for all three cells*. If the reading for one cell differs substantially from the readings for the other two it is possible that some electrolyte has been spilled or a short-circuit is occurring between the battery plates. In the latter case the battery must be returned to a service depot for attention. After taking S.G. readings, always clean the top of the battery. Electrolyte S.G. readings and their indications are as follows:

1·270–1·290 (Lucas), 1·280 (Exide)—battery *fully* charged.
1·190–1·210 (Lucas), 1·200 (Exide)—battery *half* discharged.
1·110–1·130 (Lucas), 1·110 (Exide)—battery *fully* discharged.

The above figures are given assuming that the temperature of the electrolyte is approximately 60 degrees Fahrenheit (32°C). At this temperature the battery needs charging if the S.G. reading falls to about 1·245. The S.G. readings should always be taken by yourself or at a garage if some loss of electrolyte is known to have occurred, or the general condition of the battery is suspect. They should not be taken immediately *after* topping-up the battery, as the electrolyte will then not be thoroughly mixed.

## LUCAS LAMPS AND HORNS (1955–65)

Two different types of Lucas headlamps have been fitted to Norton "Dominators" during the period 1955–65. Both types have a "pre-focus" double-filament main bulb mounted in a holder at the rear of the light-unit assembly comprising the reflector and lens which are sealed together. Only one type of stop–tail lamp has been fitted.

The headlamp and stop–tail lamp require little attention other than to keep them clean, keep all wiring connexions tight, and renew the bulbs when necessary. To ensure that a headlamp provides good illumination it is, of course, necessary to see that it is properly aligned and to maintain the battery and dynamo fitted to 1955–7 models in good condition. On 1958–63 coil-ignition models and 1962–5 Sports Special and "Atlas" models with magneto ignition, the alternator needs no maintenance.

**Lighting Switch Positions.** Three positions (*see* page 1) are provided. While riding, the dynamo or alternator output varies according to the demands made on the battery and its state of charge.

**The MCH58, MCH61 Headlamps (1955–65 Models).** These excellent Lucas headlamps are fitted to 1955–7 and 1958–65 models respectively. Both types have a "pre-focus" main bulb and a pilot or parking bulb (a push-in fit) located at the rear of the light-unit as shown in Fig. 18. Instructions for main and pilot bulb renewal are given below and suitable bulbs to use are as follows:

The double-filament "pre-focus" main bulb required for a Lucas MCH58 or MCH61 headlamp is a 6-volt 30/24-watt Lucas No. 312 or 373. The latter has a left-hand dip and is strongly recommended for use

THE LIGHTING SYSTEM (MAGNETO IGNITION) 41

in Great Britain. The pilot bulb necessary for both types of headlamp is a 6-volt 3-watt Lucas No. 988 with miniature bayonet cap.

**"Pre-focus" Main Bulb Renewal (All 1955–65 Headlamps).** Always use genuine Lucas bulbs which are specially checked to see that the filament is in the correct position to give the best results. To assist in identification, Lucas bulbs have a number marked on their caps. The correct types of

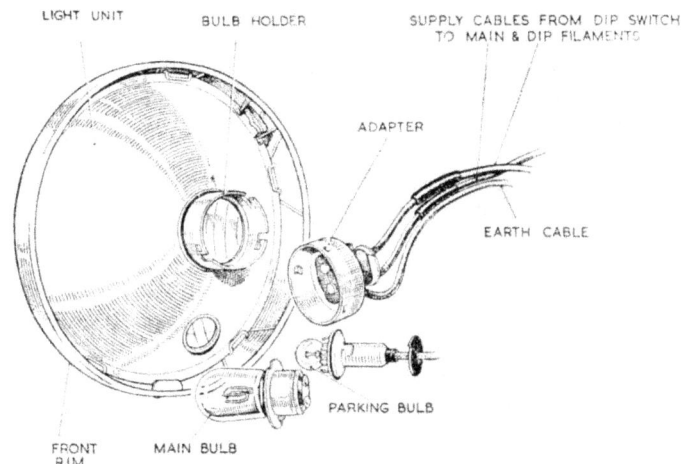

FIG. 18. THE LIGHT-UNIT, MAIN BULB AND PILOT BULB REMOVED FROM A LUCAS MCH58 OR MCH61 "PRE-FOCUS" HEADLAMP (1955–65 MODELS)

main and pilot bulbs to fit are those mentioned above. The method of fitting is as follows.

First remove the light-unit assembly comprising the lens and reflector which are sealed together and cannot be detached. Loosen the small fixing-screw at the top of the lamp rim and carefully withdraw for a short distance the rim and the attached light-unit. The wiring for the double-filament main bulb will, of course, remain attached to the adapter (see Fig. 18) and the wiring for the pilot bulb will remain connected to the holder for the pilot bulb. To remove the "pre-focus" double-filament main bulb, push the adapter inwards and turn it *anti-clockwise*, pull the bayonet-fixing adapter off, and remove the bulb from its holder in the rear of the reflector.

Fit a new Lucas No. 312 or 373 "pre-focus" bulb into the bulb holder, with the notch on its broad locating flange engaging the projection in the bulb holder. Then engage the projections on the inside of the adapter with the slots in the bulb holder and secure the adapter by turning it *clockwise* while pressing it inwards. Afterwards replace the lamp rim with the attached light-unit. Securely tighten the rim fixing-screw.

**Pilot Bulb Renewal (1955–65 Headlamps).** On all Lucas headlamps of the non-focusing type (i.e. with "pre-focus" main bulbs) the pilot bulb is fitted to a holder (*see* Fig. 18) which is a push-fit in the back of the light-unit. To renew the pilot bulb, remove the lamp rim with attached light-unit as previously described. Then pull the sprung holder out, complete with its bulb. When pulling the holder away, be careful not to lose the rubber washer. Fit a new Lucas No. 988 bulb into the holder, replace the holder (with bulb and washer) in the light-unit, and finally replace the lamp rim with attached light-unit. Secure the rim to the lamp shell with the fixing-screw.

**The Speedometer Light.** The bulb holder is accessible on removing the knurled ring. If a bulb requires renewing, fit a 6-volt, 1·8 watt (0·3 amp) bulb.

**Headlamp Alignment (All Types).** Correct alignment of a non-focusing type headlamp is essential. If correctly aligned, a Lucas headlamp should have, *with the motor-cycle carrying its normal load*, its main or driving beam projecting straight ahead and parallel with the surface of a level road. Many garages have a Lucas "Beamsetter," a scientific instrument which enables accurate beam setting to be obtained. You are advised to make use of this service.

To adjust the headlamp alignment yourself, place your Norton so that it faces a light-coloured wall about 25 feet away. Switch on the main driving-light and take vertical measurements from the centre of the headlamp and from the centre of the illuminated area on the wall to the ground. Both measurements should be equal. If they are not, loosen the two lamp securing-bolts and tilt the headlamp until the centre of the beam is truly parallel with the ground. Afterwards firmly tighten the two lamp securing-bolts.

**The 564 Stop–Tail Lamp (1955–65 Models).** This lamp, shown in Fig. 19, has a twin reflex-reflector formed in the plastic cover which is secured by two nuts. To obtain access to the double-filament bulb which has unequally positioned bayonet pins to prevent incorrect fitting, it is only necessary to remove the two nuts which secure the moulded-plastic cover. It is important not to connect the lamp leads incorrectly. The correct bulb to fit is a 6-volt, 6/18 watt, double-contact, S.B.C. Lucas No. 384.

**Cleaning Lucas Lamps.** Clean the shell of a Lucas lamp with a good car polish and clean the chromium-plated rim with a chamois leather or a

THE LIGHTING SYSTEM (MAGNETO IGNITION) 43

soft, dry duster. All dirt should, of course, first be removed. Always keep the outside of the glass of a "pre-focus" lamp absolutely clean.

**The Lighting Switch (1955–65).** This seldom gives any trouble and it is best not to disturb it without very good reason. If trouble does occur in the switch or elsewhere in the lighting circuit, the wiring diagrams in this and the next chapter may prove helpful, but if you have little electrical

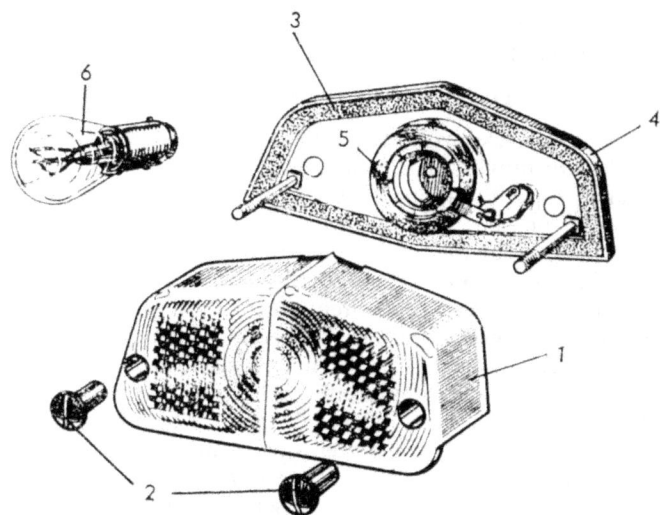

FIG. 19. THE LUCAS 564 STOP–TAIL LAMP (1955–65 MODELS)
It is impossible to fit the bulb incorrectly.

1. Plastic cover with twin reflex-reflector.
2. Cover securing-nuts.
3. Gasket.
4. Stop-tail lamp body.
5. Grommet.
6. Double-filament bulb (6/18 watt).

knowledge and do not possess a suitable voltmeter you are advised to ride to the nearest Lucas service depot.

On all "Dominator" Nortons except the 1955–7 Models 88, 99 the lighting switch and ammeter are mounted on a panel secured to the headlamp shell or are mounted on the shell itself. Where a panel is fitted, this can be detached after removing three securing screws. Where a panel is not provided, access to the lighting switch connexions is obtained on removing the headlamp rim and light-unit. The cables can be identified by colours. If you do remove the lighting switch or make any adjustments to it, *first disconnect the lead from the battery negative terminal.*

**Lucas Electric Horns.** Various types of Lucas horns have been fitted to 1955–65 Nortons. All should give prolonged service without any attention because they are very carefully adjusted by the makers and are not subjected to severe stresses. Do not assume that a horn is itself faulty because it functions irregularly or because its diaphragm ceases to vibrate.

Failure of the horn to respond effectively may be due to a short-circuit in its wiring, a loose connexion, or a discharged battery. Poor horn performance can also be caused by a slack horn-fixing bolt, or even by the vibration of some part close to the horn. To check these two last possibilities, hold the horn firmly in the hand by its bracket and test it for performance. If unsatisfactory, get the horn examined and adjusted at a Lucas service depot.

### THE WIRING CIRCUIT (1955–65)

Keep all cable connexions and terminals tight and see that all electrical leads are clear of moving parts and free from oil or grease. Also see that all leads are properly clipped or taped to prevent chafing. The wiring harness should then last for years with little attention. Where a stop–tail lamp is fitted, see that the lead connectors are themselves firmly secured by the aluminium clip on the mudguard.

If a serious fault in the wiring circuit occurs and you have neither much electrical knowledge nor a suitable voltmeter, the trouble is best diagnosed at a Lucas service depot. For the benefit of those who may wish to make any alterations to the wiring, some useful Lucas wiring diagrams are included by kind permission of Joseph Lucas Ltd. on pages 45–48 and on page 56. Before making any alteration or adjustment, however, make sure that you first *disconnect the lead from the battery negative terminal*. Unless you do this, a short-circuit with serious consequences is probable.

All cables can be identified by coloured braided insulation, coloured sleeves, or coloured plastic insulation. The colour scheme and connexions are clearly indicated in the wiring diagrams. To make a connexion to the lighting switch, bare about ¾ in. of the cable, twist the strands together, and turn back about ⅛ in. Remove the grub-screw from the appropriate terminal, and insert the wire in the terminal post. Then replace and tighten the grub-screw.

### SLEEVE COLOURS FOR WIRING (Figs. 21–23)

| | | |
|---|---|---|
| B. Black | L. Light | R. Red |
| D. Dark | M. Medium | S. Slate |
| G. Green | N. Brown | W. White |
| K. Pink | P. Purple | Y. Yellow |

To make a connexion to the terminals of a dynamo or C.V.C. unit, slacken the securing screw or screws on the terminal block and remove the clamping plate. Then withdraw the metal ferrules from each terminal.

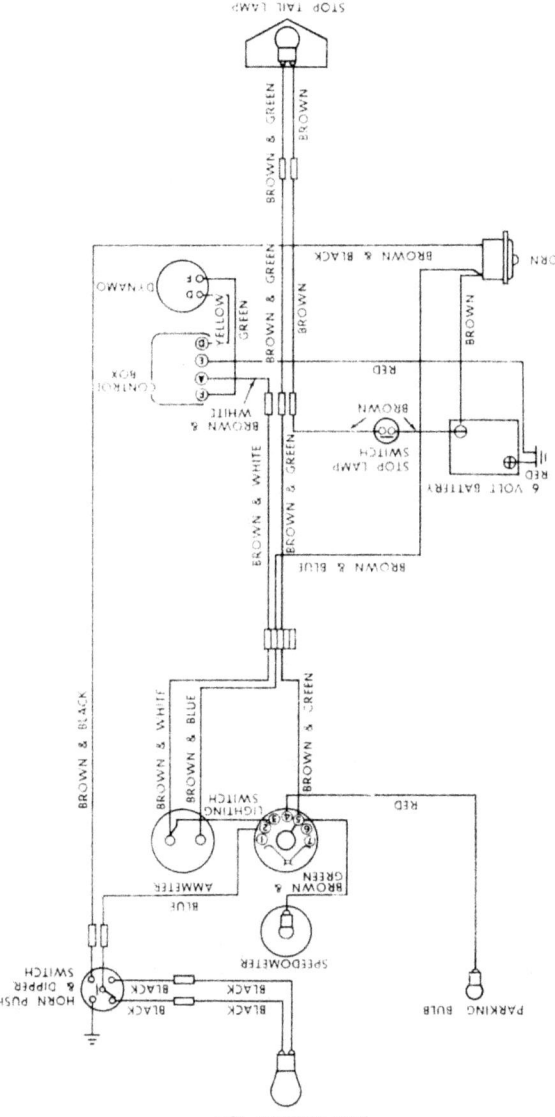

Fig. 20. Wiring Diagram for Lucas Dynamo Lighting Equipment Fitted to the 1955–7 Standard Models 88, 99

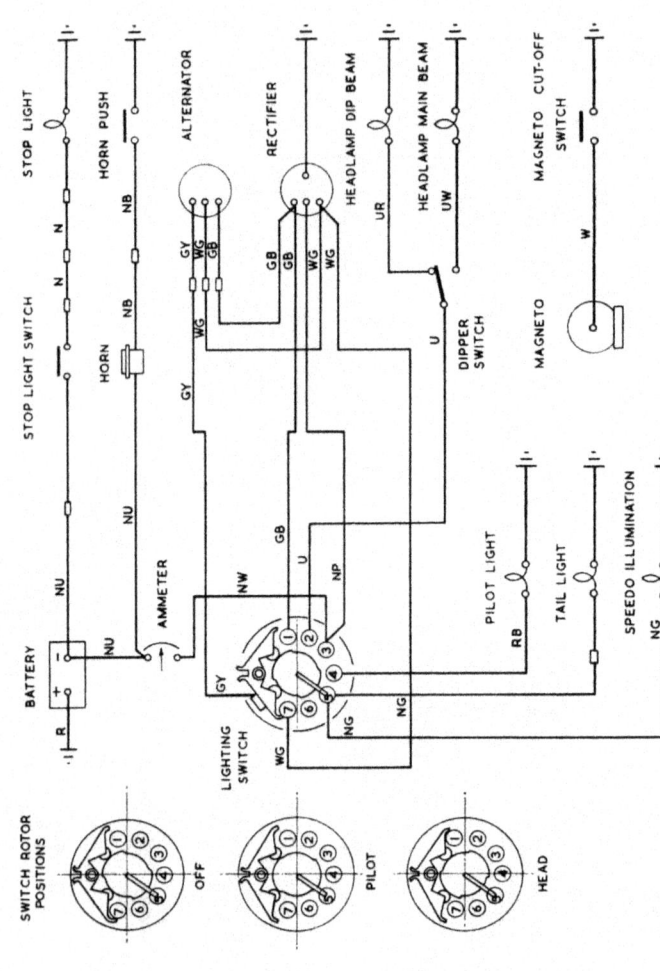

Fig. 21. Wiring Diagram for Lucas Lighting Equipment Fitted to the 1962-3 Magneto-Ignition Models 88SS, 99SS, 650SS

For key to coloured sleeves see page 44.

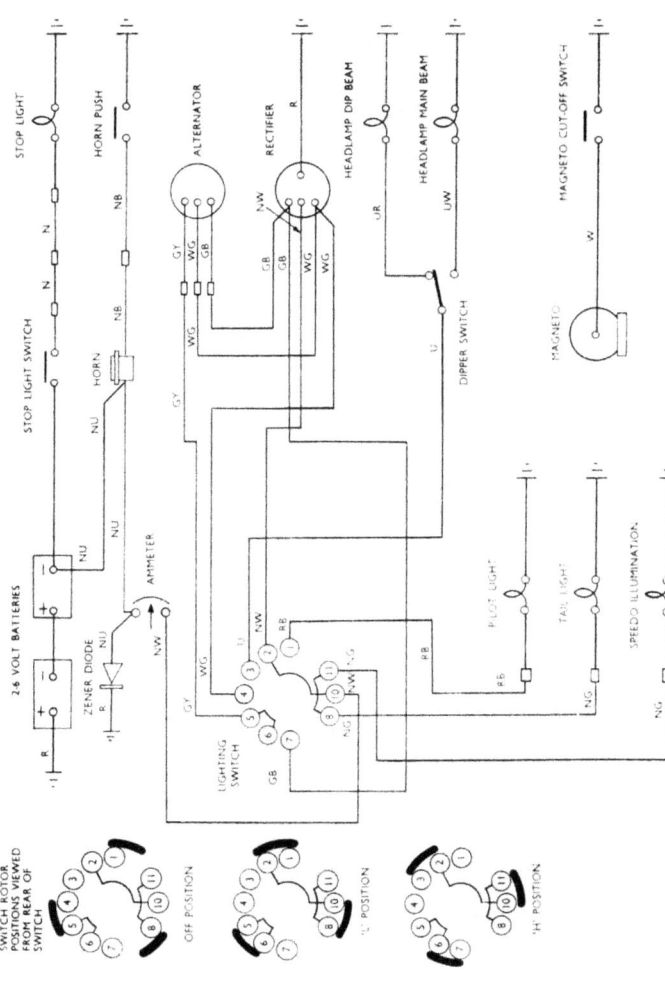

Fig. 22. Wiring Diagram for Lucas Lighting Equipment Fitted to the 1964–5 Magneto-Ignition Model 88SS

On later versions of Model 88SS the diode is connected to the NW terminal of the ammeter and the diode colour is brown/white. For key to coloured sleeves see page 44.

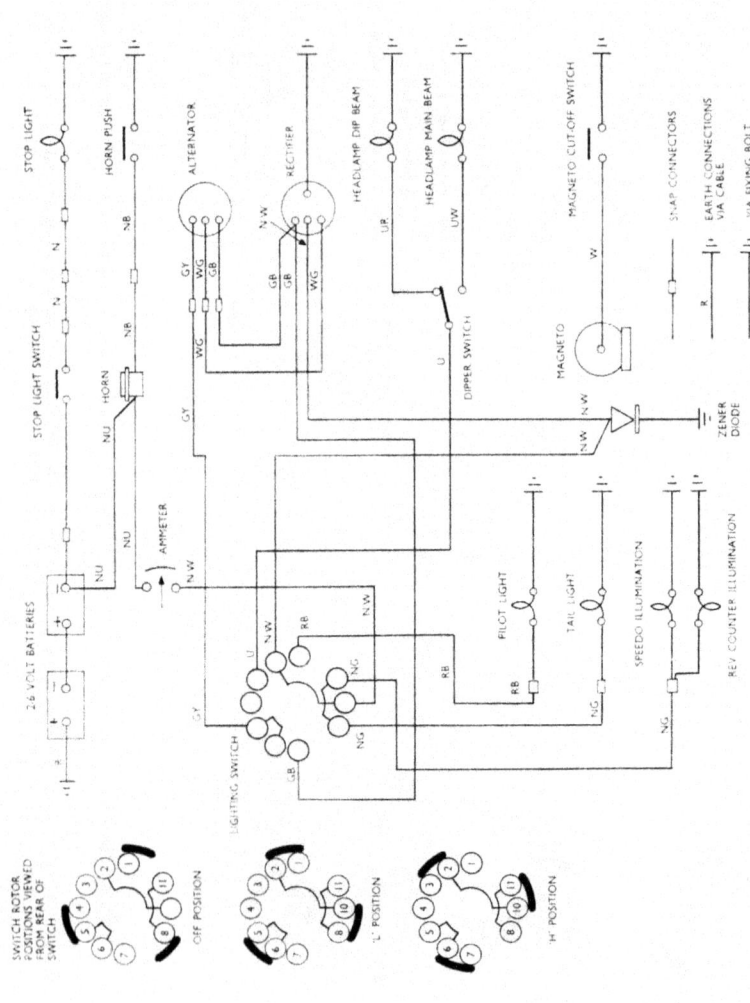

Fig. 23. Wiring Diagram for Lucas Lighting Equipment Fitted to the 1964-5 Magneto-Ignition Models 650SS, 750 "Atlas"

For key to coloured sleeves see page 44.

Pass about 1 in. of cable through the holes in the clamping plate and bare the ends for $\frac{3}{8}$ in. Fit the metal ferrules over the cables, bend back the wire strands over the ferrules and push them well home into their terminals. Afterwards tighten down the clamping plate firmly. The cables connected to the "D" and "F" terminals of the dynamo and C.V.C. units must not be reversed.

**Snap Connectors.** Rubber-covered push-and-pull connexions are included at many points in the wiring circuit. Disconnect a snap connector by pulling the two metal halves apart. When re-connecting it hold the metal nipple soldered to the cable end with cable pliers. Hold the rubber-covered portion with the fingers and press the nipple home with the pliers. Make sure afterwards that the complete connector is fully covered by the rubber sleeve.

# 5 The lighting-ignition (coil) system

ALL 1958–63 Norton "Dominators" except Special Sports (SS) models and the 1964–5 750 cc "Atlas" have coil ignition and, unlike the magneto-ignition models, they have a Lucas a.c. lighting–ignition system in which the lighting and ignition equipment are *combined* and not independent.

The 1958–63 a.c. equipment comprises a Lucas headlamp with combined lighting and ignition switch, an alternator, rectifier, battery, ignition coil, Lucas 18D-2 contact-breaker distributor unit and, of course, a pair of sparking plugs. The alternator, rectifier, and battery are used for lighting *and* ignition.

**An Outline of the Lucas System.** The generator, an alternator fitted to the near-side flywheel mainshaft, during rotation of its rotor produces alternating (a.c.) current. This a.c. current is converted by the rectifier into uni-directional or direct (d.c.) current before it charges the battery. The rectifier in effect acts like a non-return valve. Current from the battery is fed direct to the lamps when the lighting switch is switched on. With the engine running and the ignition switched on, current is also fed from the battery to both sparking plugs through the contact-breaker, ignition coil, and distributor. The contact-breaker and the ignition coil convert low-tension current into high-tension current at the appropriate time when the contacts of the contact-breaker open, and the distributor sees to it that the H.T. current is fed to the correct sparking plug when the cylinder concerned is due to fire. This is, of course, only a very brief outline of the Lucas system.

### USE OF SYSTEM (1958–63) MODELS)

**The Lighting Switch and Ignition Key.** The lighting switch has three positions (*see* page 1) and the detachable ignition key is mounted in the centre of it as shown in Fig. 2. The combined switch is rather complicated and it is not advisable to attempt to dismantle it. When the lighting switch is turned to the "L" position with the engine running, two pairs of alternator coils are disconnected and only the third pair is in use; current is thus provided for trickle-charging the battery through the rectifier and also energizes the ignition coil. With the lighting switch in the "H" position the alternator output is increased by connecting all three pairs of coils in parallel, thereby providing current for the headlamp, stop–tail lamp, and the speedometer light, as well as for ignition and simultaneously trickle-charging the battery.

**The Dipper Switch.** Sticking of this switch prevents immediate change-over from one of the headlamp filaments to the other, and can be dangerous. The dipper switch is best connected so that the dipped beam is in use when the switch lever is lowered. Occasionally lubricate the switch (*see* page 29).

**Emergency Starting (1958–63 Models).** As has been stated on page 2, the ignition key has an emergency starting ("EMG") position for use if the battery is discharged. When the ignition key is moved to the "EMG" position the ignition coil is connected direct to the alternator. It is then possible to start the engine without the assistance of the battery. As soon as the engine starts, the ignition key must be turned to the "IGN" position.

When operating the kick-starter with the ignition key in the "EMG" position it may be necessary to use considerably more force than is normally required. If the ignition timing for any reason varies only slightly from the correct timing, emergency starting may be impossible. In this case, try a push-start with second gear engaged and the ignition key in the "IGN" position.

If the alternator leads have been changed over to increase dynamo output (*see* below) a start with the ignition key in the "EMG" position may be impracticable. The remedy is to change back the leads temporarily or to try a push-start.

**Increasing Alternator Output (1958–65 Models).** If the battery becomes badly discharged through prolonged slow riding in traffic or during running-in, or because of parking with lights on for extensive periods, or after a sidecar is attached, you can increase the alternator output by making a simple alteration to the wiring.

The leads from the alternator after emerging from the oil-bath chain case join the main electrical harness by means of a three-way snap connector. This is usually clipped to the H.T. leads where they leave the distributor or else higher up near the top of the battery box. The lead colours are: light green or green and white; dark green or green and black; and green and yellow. Disconnect the dark green or green and black, and the green and yellow leads and attach them to the two connectors after reversing the leads. In other words, connect the green and black alternator cable to the green and yellow harness cable; connect the green and black harness cable to the green and yellow alternator cable.

After making the above alteration the ammeter should, with the lighting switch in the "OFF" position, indicate approximately twice the previous alternator output. With the lighting switch turned to the "L" or "H" position, however, the output remains unchanged.

Note that when riding a solo machine for a long distance during daylight after increasing the alternator output as previously described, the battery may become overcharged, and this may damage the battery and also parts of the motor-cycle through acid spillage. Whenever a sidecar is permanently attached to the motor-cycle it is desirable to increase the alternator output, otherwise the current consumption of the sidecar lamps will not be compensated for, and the battery will slowly discharge.

## MAINTENANCE OF LIGHTING–IGNITION SYSTEM

**The Alternator (1958–65 Models).** The Lucas RM19 alternator requires no maintenance other than occasional attention to the few small points mentioned on page 34.

Note that there should always be at least 0·005 in. clearance between the rotor and the pole pieces on the stator. Check this clearance whenever you have occasion to remove and replace the stator. Its removal is, of course, very rarely necessary. Observe that the stator must be fitted with the lead take-off side towards the primary chain and *not* towards the outer portion of the oil-bath chain case.

To remove the rotor which is keyed to the near-side flywheel mainshaft (*see* Fig. 45), remove its securing nut and pull the rotor off. It may be necessary to remove the stator (secured by three nuts and fan disc washers) if the rotor is tight on its shaft.

When the rotor is removed it is quite unnecessary to fit keepers to the rotor poles. Wipe off any metal swarf which may have collected on the pole tips, and place the rotor in a clean place.

It is possible to fit the stator either way round into the spigot recess, but it will only function satisfactorily in one position. It is correctly fitted when the edge from which the leads emerge is innermost or away from the the outer portion of the oil-bath chain case.

**The Battery.** See pages 35–40.

**The Rectifier.** No attention is necessary to this except to keep its connexions tight and the unit securely fixed to the motor-cycle (*see* page 34).

**The Ignition Coil (1958–63 Models).** A Lucas type MA6 ignition coil is secured on 1958–9 models to a bracket welded to the inside of the off-side tank rail on the frame. On 1960–3 models the ignition coil is transversely positioned on the frame cross-tube at the rear of the petrol tank. As in the case of the rectifier, the coil requires no attention except occasional checking that its terminals and mounting are clean and tight.

## THE LIGHTING-IGNITION (COIL) SYSTEM 53

**Sparking Plugs.** See pages 60-3 for correct types and maintenance.

**Lamps.** All 1958-63 coil-ignition "Dominators" have a Lucas MCH61 headlamp with a "pre-focus" main bulb, and a Lucas 564 stop-tail lamp. Bulb renewal is occasionally necessary. The correct Lucas bulbs to fit and how to fit them are dealt with on pages 40-2.

**The Horn.** No maintenance is necessary. If trouble occurs, act in accordance with the advice given on page 43.

**To Check Contact-breaker Gap (1958-63 Models).** Check the gap of the Lucas contact-breaker on a new machine after covering 500 miles and subsequently every 6,000 miles. Remove the distributor cover from the Lucas 18D-2 contact-breaker distributor unit, and also both sparking plugs to enable the engine to be rotated freely and slowly.

Slowly turn the engine over by hand until one lobe of the cam is directly under the heel of the contact-breaker lever (the rocker arm). In this position the contacts are wide open and the gap between them should be 0·014 in.–0·016 in. Check the existing gap by inserting a clean 0·015 in. feeler gauge between the contacts. It should just slide in without pressure. The cam lobes are of high grade steel and do not wear. It should therefore not be necessary to check the gap with the rocker-arm heel fully raised by the other lobe of the cam. If the contact-breaker gap is found to be incorrect, make the required adjustment as follows.

With the engine turned to the position giving maximum contact separation, loosen slightly the fixed contact plate-securing screw (*see* Fig. 24). Then insert a screwdriver between the two projections on the base plate and the notch in the fixed-contact plate and adjust the position of the plate until the contact-breaker gap is found to be correct. Afterwards re-tighten the fixed contact plate-securing screw and again check the gap between the contacts by inserting a 0·015 in. feeler gauge. Finally replace the distributor cover and both sparking plugs.

**Cleaning, Oiling Contact-breaker Distributor Unit (1958-63 Models).** The Lucas 18D-2 unit should be cleaned and oiled when checking the contact-breaker gap every 6,000 miles.

Remove and clean the distributor cover. It is easily damaged and must be handled with great care. Pay special attention to the spaces between the metal electrodes in the cover, and check that the small carbon brush moves freely in its holder.

Withdraw the rotor arm (*see* Fig. 24) and unscrew the two contact-breaker base plate securing-screws. Then remove the base plate and apply some clean engine oil to the automatic-advance mechanism, paying special attention to its pivots. Afterwards replace the base plate, tighten its two securing screws, and replace the rotor arm.

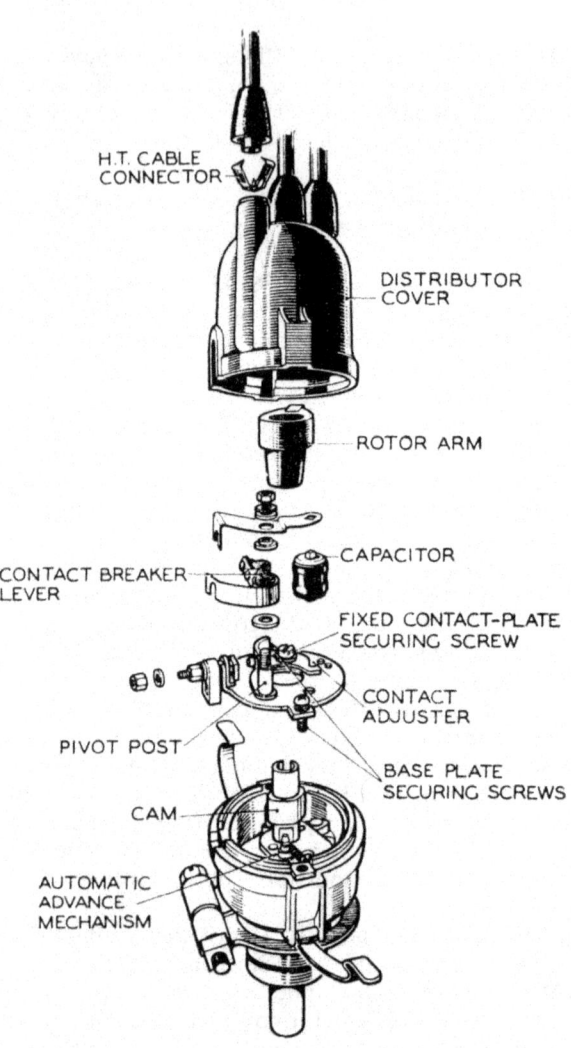

Fig. 24. Exploded View of Lucas 18D-2 Contact-Breaker Distributor Unit

This unit is positioned horizontally behind the cylinder block on all 1958–63 coil-ignition models and is chain-driven from the intermediate timing gear.

## THE LIGHTING–IGNITION (COIL) SYSTEM

Carefully examine the condition of the contact-breaker contacts. If their surfaces have a grey, frosted appearance with no blackening or pitting present, it is generally sufficient to clean the contacts with a cloth moistened with petrol. Make sure that there is no dirt, oil, or grease on or near the contacts. Dirty contacts rapidly become burnt and pitted.

If the contacts are found to be very slightly blackened or pitted it is generally possible to clean both contacts satisfactorily with some *very fine* emery cloth inserted between them. If considerable blackening and pitting is present, it is advisable to remove the rocker arm carrying the moving contact. Then clean and polish both contacts most carefully and thoroughly, using a fine carborundum stone, silicon carbide paper, or a piece of very fine emery cloth. Continue cleaning the contacts until all blackening and pitting disappears and the contact surfaces are smooth all over. Be careful to keep the contact faces "square", and avoid removing excessive metal. After cleaning the contacts remove all traces of metal dust and abrasive with a clean cloth moistened with petrol.

If a reasonable amount of facing up fails to restore the contact faces to normal, fit a new pair of contacts. When cleaning is completed, replace the rocker arm carrying the moving contact. Before doing this smear the cam and rocker-arm pivot lightly with some clean engine oil. Finally check the contact-breaker gap and if necessary make an adjustment (*see* page 53).

**Removal of Contact-breaker Distributor Unit (1958–63 Models).** The Lucas 18D-2 unit is chain driven from the intermediate timing gear, its driving sprocket being located on the distributor spindle by a parallel peg whose removal enables the sprocket to be withdrawn. Behind the sprocket there is on most engines a tubular spacer and copper washer on the spindle. See that these are not misplaced. Note that the washer goes on the spindle first.

Removal of a single bolt or set-screw holding the clamping flange to the inside of the timing-cover extension enables the complete contact-breaker distributor unit to be extracted from the housing, provided that the distributor cover carrying the sparking plug and coil leads has first been removed by springing off the two clips securing it to the distributor body.

It may also be necessary to remove the low-tension connexion to the contact-breaker so that the latter can be turned as it is withdrawn in order that the bolt in the clamp will clear the engine plates. Alternatively release the clamping bolt and withdraw the unit, leaving the clip attached to the housing by the set-screw. For routine maintenance it is, of course, not necessary to remove the Lucas 18D-2 unit.

**Ignition Timing (1958–63 Models).** The ignition timing used and decided upon after much experiment by the makers should *under no circumstances*

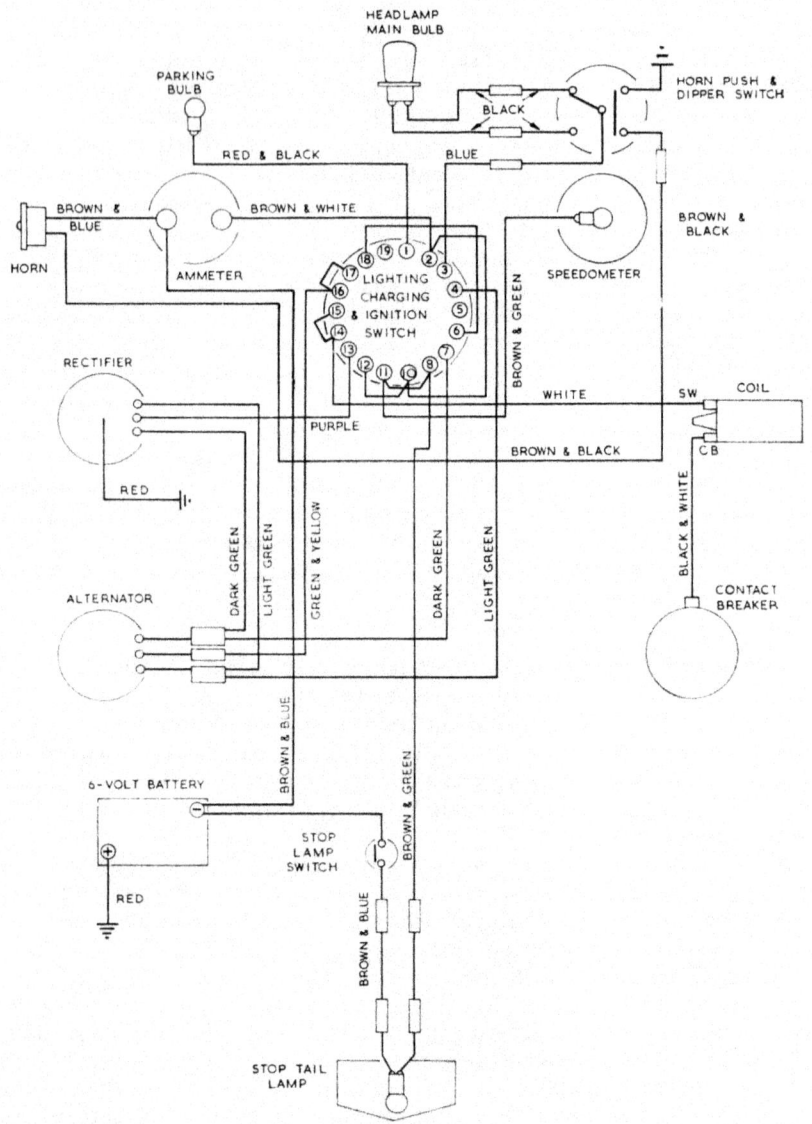

FIG. 25. WIRING DIAGRAM FOR LUCAS A.C. LIGHTING–IGNITION EQUIPMENT FITTED TO ALL 1958–63 COIL-IGNITION MODELS

be altered. It is set to give the best engine performance under all conditions. Retiming is not necessary unless the distributor driving-chain (the narrower of the two chains) has been removed or the sprockets in the timing case have been disturbed. Instructions for retiming the ignition are given on page 87.

Note that a slack distributor driving-chain will upset the ignition timing. The chain should have a total up-and-down movement of $\tfrac{3}{16}$ in. on one chain run at its tightest point. If an adjustment is necessary, slacken the two Allen nuts near the upper edge of the distributor adapter. A tap with a mallet or gentle leverage will pivot the assembly about the bottom stud enough to allow for normal adjustment of the chain.

**Renewing H.T. Cables.** Cracked or perished H.T. cables should be renewed by fitting 7 mm. P.V.C. or Neoprene covered vulcanized-rubber insulated ignition cables. The leads for the ignition coil and distributor have clamped-on connectors with three spikes. It is often possible to remove these from old leads and fit them to new ones, but if the connectors are in doubtful condition, renew them as well as the high-tension leads.

**The Wiring Circuit.** Observe the general advice given on page 44. On no account make any alterations to the wiring or disconnect cables without first disconnecting the lead from the battery *negative* terminal. A wiring diagram applicable to all 1958–63 coil-ignition models is shown in Fig. 25.

# 6 General maintenance

> **NOTE**
>
> THIS chapter contains full maintenance instructions for all 1955–65 "Dominator" Nortons excluding those matters already dealt with in detail in Chapters 2–4. For the reader's convenience appropriate cross-references are included.

**Spares.** For obvious reasons major overhaul such as stripping-down the engine for bearing renewal, etc., is preferably undertaken by a competent dealer. Unfortunately, Norton Villiers Ltd. are no longer able to handle service and overhaul of these machines, nor do they supply parts.

There are, however, many reputable firms in the United Kingdom who can supply Norton spares over the counter or by mail, c.o.d. Some handle the repair of Norton engines and machines. You can obtain a list from Norton Villiers Ltd., of North Way, Walworth Industrial Estate, Andover, Hants., or peruse the classified advertisements in magazines such as *Motor Cycle* and *Motor Cycle Mechanics*.

Among London firms who quickly supply spares c.o.d. may be mentioned the following: Joe Francis Motors Ltd., 340 Footscray Road, S.E.9; Gus Kuhn Motors, 275 Clapham Road, Stockwell, S.W.9; and Taylor Matterson, 74 Bedford Hill, S.W.12.

**The Engine and Frame Numbers.** You will find the *engine number* of your mount located on the *transmission side of the crankcase below the cylinder-block flange*. The *frame number* is stamped on the *left hand side of the petrol tank mounting lug where the tube passes through*, or on the featherbed frame models *on the near-side frame gusset* below the battery box.

### CLEANING, ETC.

**Cleaning Enamelled Parts.** Do not attempt to remove mud from enamelled surfaces when caked and dry, as this is likely to spoil them. If available, use a hose to soak the mud off. Before directing a stream of water on to very dirty surfaces it is advisable first to smear the surfaces over with a cleaning compound. Be careful not to allow any water to get inside vulnerable parts such as the carburettor, dynamo, magneto, or contact-breaker distributor unit. Where a hose is not available, soak the mud and then disperse it with plenty of clean water, using a sponge and pail.

When you have removed all dirt, dry the enamelled surfaces with a chamois leather, and afterwards polish them with soft dusters and some good wax polish or a proprietary polish such as "Karpol."

Those who ride in dry weather only can keep a machine in almost showroom condition by merely rubbing the enamel over with a paraffin-damped rag, followed by a dry, soft duster.

**Cleaning the Chromium.** The normal method of removing tarnish (salt deposits) is to clean the surfaces regularly with a damp chamois leather and then polish them with soft dusters. Never use liquid metal polish or paste, because this will wear down the thin surface. It is permissible, however, to use a good chromium-cleaning compound such as "Belco."

**To Reduce Tarnishing.** It is a good plan during the winter to wipe over occasionally all chromium surfaces with a soft cloth soaked in a proprietary anti-tarnish preparation such as "Tekall," obtainable in $\frac{1}{2}$ pint and 1 pint tins.

**The Engine and Gearbox.** Scour all filth from the lower part of the engine and gearbox, using stiff brushes and paraffin. Clean all aluminium-alloy and bright surfaces with a rag damped in paraffin, assisted by brushes where necessary.

Keep the cylinder head and cylinder-block fins clean. If the enamel has worn away from the cylinder-block fins, clean the fins with a stiff brush dipped in paraffin and then paint the fins with some proprietary cylinder black. Rusted fins, besides looking shabby, cause some appreciable loss in heat dispersion.

**Run-in a New Engine With Great Care.** Where a new or a re-conditioned engine is concerned, ride with great care during the first 1,000 miles. Avoid large throttle openings, excessive speed, and make full use of the gearbox. A summary of correct running-in procedure is given on page 4.

**Check Nuts and Bolts for Tightness.** During running-in some "bedding down" of parts is inevitable and after running for a few hundred miles it is advisable to apply spanners to the various external nuts and bolts. Pay special attention to the nuts securing the cylinder block, the cylinder-head nuts and bolts, the engine mounting nuts, and all pipe unions. The wise motor-cyclist continues after running-in is completed to make periodical quick checks for tightness of various external nuts and bolts.

**The Amal Carburettor.** Instructions for making a slow-running adjustment on the "monobloc" type carburettor are given on pages 6–7 of Chapter II. Carburettor maintenance is dealt with on pages 9–13.

**Correct Lubrication.** This and regular cleaning of the filters in the dry sump lubrication system are of *vital* importance. Engine lubrication (including the lubrication of dynamos, magnetos, and contact-breaker distributor units) is comprehensively covered on pages 14–24 of Chapter III. For instructions on the lubrication of the various motor-cycle parts, see pages 24–29 in the same chapter.

**The Lucas Lighting Equipment.** Chapter IV gives maintenance instructions for dynamo lighting equipment fitted to 1955–7 models with separate magneto ignition. It also gives maintenance instructions for the alternator and rectifier provided on 1962–5 Sports Special (SS) and 650 cc "Atlas" models with magneto ignition, and all types of Lucas batteries, lamps, and horns fitted to 1955–65 models. The combined lighting and ignition equipment used on all 1958–63 coil-ignition models is fully covered in Chapter V.

## SPARKING PLUGS AND MAGNETOS

**Recommended Sparking Plugs.** To ensure easy starting, a cool-running engine, and good all-round performance it is essential always to use sparking plugs of the make and type recommended by Norton Motors Ltd. The makes recommended are K.L.G., Lodge and Champion and suitable types to fit are as follows:

*All 1955–63 Standard, De Luxe Models.* The sparking plugs suitable for fitting to the *aluminium-alloy* cylinder heads of *all* these models must be of the 14 mm. ($\frac{3}{4}$ in. reach) type. Those recommended by Norton Motors Ltd. are: the detachable-type K.L.G. FE75, DFE75 or FE80; the non-detachable type Lodge 2HLN; and the non-detachable type Champion N5.

*1962–5 Sports Special Models.* All these models also have *aluminium-alloy* cylinder heads requiring 14 mm. ($\frac{3}{4}$ in. reach) type sparking plugs. To obtain maximum engine efficiency Norton Motors Ltd. advise the fitting of a pair of the following plugs: a detachable-type K.L.G. FE80 or FE100; a non-detachable type Lodge 2HLN or 3HLN; or a non-detachable type Champion N4.

*1964–5 740 cc "Atlas" Models.* Norton Motors Ltd. specifically recommend the fitting of a pair of 14 mm. ($\frac{3}{4}$ in. reach) K.L.G. FE75 sparking plugs. Alternatively DFE75 "Super" K.L.G. plugs can be fitted to the *aluminium-alloy* cylinder head.

# GENERAL MAINTENANCE

**The Sparking Plug Gap.** To ensure easy starting and to maintain efficient fuel combustion it is advisable to check the gap between the electrodes of both sparking plugs about every 2,000 miles. The effective life of a sparking plug is considerable, but the points of the electrodes gradually burn away and it is necessary to regap them. Norton Motors Ltd. recommend a gap of 0·015 in–0·020 in. (0·018 in.–0·022 in. on the 750 cc "Atlas") for engines with magneto ignition, and 0·020 in–0·025 in. for engines with coil ignition. Check the gap with a suitable feeler gauge,

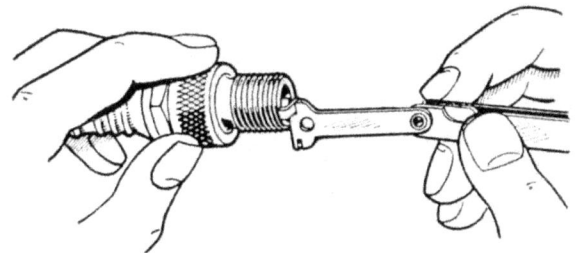

FIG. 26. THE SAFEST WAY TO RE-GAP A PLUG

The Champion tool shown includes feeler gauges for checking the sparking plug gap.

or a wire gauge if the points are not very accessible. The gauge should just enter without having to spring the points.

When adjusting the gap between the centre and outer (earth) electrodes never attempt to bend or tap the centre electrode. Use a small pair of snipe-nose pliers, or better still, a Lodge or Champion re-gapping tool as shown in Fig. 26 to bend the outer electrode(s). Tapping is not recommended.

**Cleaning the Sparking Plugs.** When running-in a new or rebored engine it is advisable to remove and clean both sparking plugs every 500 miles. After running-in it should not be necessary to clean the sparking plugs more often than about every 3,000 miles, assuming that carburation is correct and there is no tendency for the plugs to oil up. It is, of course, possible to clean any type of sparking plug quickly if found to be only slightly dirty or oily. Brush the points with a wire brush, rub them slightly with some smooth emery cloth, and then flush out the plug with petrol. Alternatively screw the plug into a proprietary cleaner (containing steel wires and petrol) and shake it. Thorough cleaning is usually necessary about every 3,000 miles, and should be done as described below.

**Non-detachable Type Plugs.** Sparking plugs such as the Lodge 2HLN or Champion N5 which cannot be dismantled should be thoroughly cleaned on an "air-blast" unit at a nearby garage. In a few minutes the plug is thoroughly cleaned of all deposits, washed, subjected to a high-pressure air line, and finally tested for sparking at a pressure exceeding 100 lb per sq in. K.L.G. plugs can be similarly dealt with.

**Detachable-type Plugs.** Sparking plugs such as the K.L.G. FE75 or FE80 can be dismantled for thorough cleaning, as shown in Fig. 27.

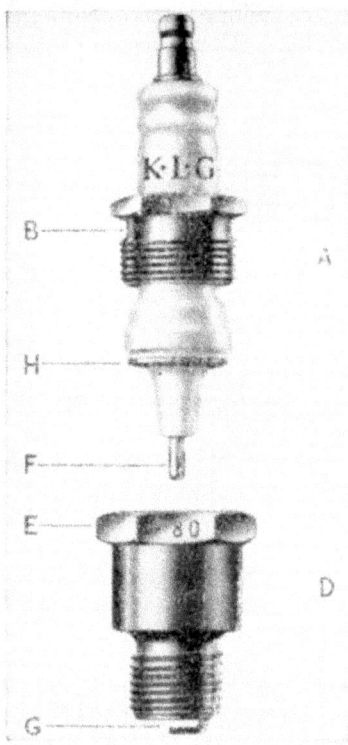

FIG. 27. DETACHABLE-TYPE SPARKING PLUG (K.L.G.) DISMANTLED FOR THOROUGH CLEANING

To dismantle a detachable-type plug, grip the larger hexagon of the plug body in a vice or with a box spanner. If you use a vice, be very careful not to exert any pressure on its hexagon faces. Then with a box or ring spanner unscrew the gland nut (*B*), being careful not to distort the integral metal body. Now detach the centre electrode (*F*) with its insulation, comprising the insulated electrode assembly (*A*), from the gland nut. See that you do not lose the internal sealing-washer (*H*).

Clean the plug insulation with a cloth soaked in petrol or paraffin and remove any hard deposits with *fine* glass-paper. Do not scrape them off.

## GENERAL MAINTENANCE

The internal sealing-washer ($H$) is responsible for preventing gas leakage through the plug and must be in perfect condition. The same applies to the surfaces in contact with it.

Thoroughly clean the plug body and gland nut, scraping off all deposits with a wire brush, afterwards rinsing the parts in petrol. The inside of the plug body can conveniently be cleaned with emery tape wrapped round a screwdriver. Unlike the gland nut, it often gets very dirty. Clean and polish the points of the centre and outside (earth) electrodes ($F$) and ($G$) with some *very fine* emery cloth.

Make sure that no dirt or grit is lodged between the body of the plug and the insulation, and especially on the internal sealing-washer and the contacting faces. Smear a little thin oil on the washer and check that it seats properly when assembling the plug. Also see that the centre electrode and insulation are positioned centrally in the plug body. When replacing and tightening the gland nut, use a box or ring spanner and avoid using excessive pressure. Finally check the sparking plug gap (*see* page 61).

**Replacing the Sparking Plugs.** Before doing this, renew the copper washers if flattened or worn. Also clean the plug threads throughly with a wire brush if this has not already been done. Screw home both plugs by hand as far as possible and always use a box spanner for final tightening. To assist future removal of the plugs it is a good plan to coat their threads with some graphite paste or "Oil Dag" before fitting them.

**Rotating-armature Magnetos (1955–65 Models).** On all magneto-ignition models except Sports Special and 750 cc "Atlas" models a Lucas K2F magneto is fitted. The SS and "Atlas" models have a Lucas type K2FC magneto. Both types of magneto are similar and require the same maintenance. Every 3,000 miles lubricate the cam ring, the rocker arm, the rocker arm pivot, and the contact-breaker spring as described on pages 21–4 in Chapter III. Proper lubrication necessitates removal of the contact-breaker from the magneto-armature spindle. *Each time you remove the contact-breaker for lubrication examine the contacts for blackening and pitting.* If the contacts need cleaning, deal with them as described on page 55 for the Lucas 18D-2 contact-breaker distributor unit fitted to coil-ignition models. Thorough cleaning is unlikely to be needed except at 6,000 mile intervals when the magneto itself should be cleaned and inspected as described below.

Remove the contact-breaker cover and also the high-tension pick-up mouldings. Clean thoroughly the inside and outside of the magneto, using a clean, dry, fluffless cloth. Moisten the cloth with petrol to remove any grease from the H.T. pick-up mouldings and the contacts of the contact-breaker. Check that the pick-up brush moves freely in its holder. If the brush is worn to $\frac{1}{8}$ in. above the shoulder, renew it. Clean the slip-ring track and the flanges by pressing the cloth on them while slowly rotating the engine by hand. Also check that the gaskets between the pick-up mouldings and the body of the magneto are in good condition.

**Check Magneto Contact-breaker Gap Every 3,000 Miles.** Two types of contact-breaker have been fitted to Lucas K2F and K2FC magnetos, an earlier type and a later type (*see* Figs. 9, 10). For both types of contact-breaker the correct gap between their contacts when wide open is 0·012 in. plus or minus 0·001 in. Every 3,000 miles remove the contact-breaker cover and turn the engine over slowly by hand until the magneto contacts

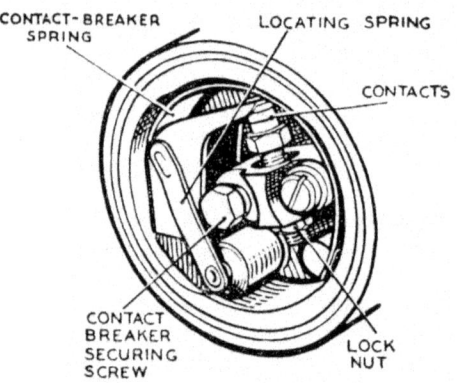

Fig. 28. The Earlier Type Contact-Breaker on the Lucas K2F K2FC Magneto

are wide open. Then insert a suitable feeler gauge between them. It should just slide in without springing the contacts. If an adjustment is necessary, make this as described below.

Where an earlier type contact-breaker is concerned, slacken the lock-nut which secures the fixed contact (*see* Fig. 28) and then turn the contact by its hexagon head until insertion of a feeler gauge shows the gap between the contacts to be correct. Then re-tighten the lock-nut and again check the gap.

On all magnetos with the later type contact-breaker to adjust the gap between the contacts when wide open, slacken the fixed contact-plate securing screw (*see* Fig. 29) which passes through a hole in the plate, and with a screwdriver move the fixed-contact plate until a feeler gauge shows the gap between the contacts to be correct. Then tighten the screw and re-check the gap.

**Contact-breakers Are Interchangeable.** If you have a magneto provided with the earlier type contact-breaker you can, if you wish, fit the later type contact-breaker in its place. You must, however, secure it with a shorter straight-shanked screw (*see* Fig. 10) instead of the larger screw which has a 17 degree taper for $\frac{3}{16}$ in. below its head, and *check ignition timing*.

**The Automatic Timing Control.** All Lucas rotating-armature magnetos fitted to Norton "Dominator" models incorporate an automatic timing control mechanism of the centrifugal type. When the magneto spindle is stationary the weights (*see* Fig. 30) are in the closed position and the magneto is retarded for starting. As its speed increases, centrifugal force acting on the weights overcomes the restraining influence of the control

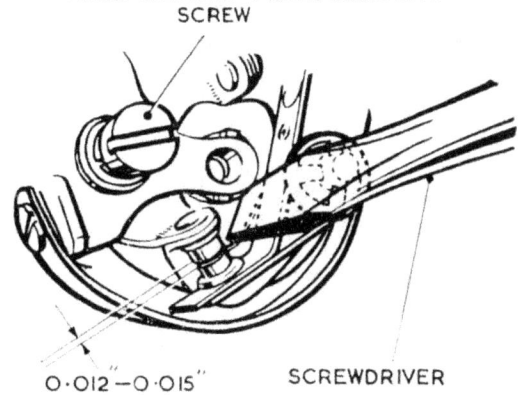

FIG. 29. ADJUSTING THE GAP OF LATER TYPE CONTACT-BREAKER ON THE LUCAS K2F, K2FC MAGNETO (*see also* FIG. 10)

springs and the weights move outwards, causing relative movement to occur between the magneto driving-gear and the magneto spindle. This automatically advances the timing.

The automatic timing control is enclosed in the timing chest of the engine and is automatically lubricated. No maintenance is normally necessary, but it is important to maintain at least $\frac{3}{16}$ in. whip in the magneto driving-chain. A tight chain tends to upset the normal functioning of the A.T.C. mechanism. About every two years, or when the engine requires a general overhaul, it is advisable to have the magneto dismantled at a Lucas Service Depot. The armature bearings can then be re-packed with grease and the weights, springs, and toggles of the centrifugal timing control inspected and lubricated.

**Magneto Removal.** On all 1955–65 models the removal of the magneto, where fitted, is quite simple. First remove the timing cover as described on page 84. Next unscrew the centre nut which secures the automatic timing-control unit. Unscrew the nut until the unit is pulled off the magneto armature-shaft. Then remove the three nuts which secure the magneto mounting-flange to the crankcase. Finally disconnect the two H.T. leads and withdraw the magneto.

**Renewing H.T. Cables.** When renewing cracked or perished high-tension cables, use 7 mm. P.V.C. or Neoprene-covered vulcanized rubber-insulated ignition cable. Pull back the rubber shroud (where fitted) and unscrew the moulded terminal from the pick-up moulding. Remove the split metal washer and moulded terminal from the defective cable. Prepare the new

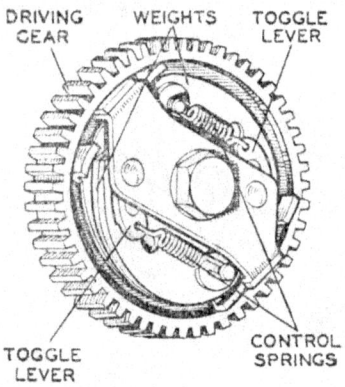

Fig. 30. The Automatic Timing Control on Lucas K2F, K2FC Magnetos

cable by cutting back the insulation for about $\frac{1}{4}$ in. Thread the cable through the rubber shroud (where fitted) and the moulded terminal. Pass the cable conductor through the metal washer and bend back the strands radially. Finally screw the moulded terminal into the pick-up moulding.

### VALVE CLEARANCES

It is advisable to check and if necessary adjust the clearances between the ends of the four valve stems and the adjusters on the overhead rockers every 1,500 miles, except in the case of a new or re-conditioned engine where the clearances should be checked after covering about 250 miles. Always check the clearances after grinding-in the valves.

**Incorrect Valve Clearances.** These affect the lift of the valves and also the valve timing. Excessive clearances result in reduced valve lift and late opening of the valves. It is unlikely to damage the valves but causes mechanical noise and some reduction in power output. Insufficient clearances, however, besides causing poor engine compression and performance, can cause actual burning of the valves through gas leakage past them during the combustion of fuel. The experienced motor-cyclist can generally tell by the feel and sound of his engine whether the valve clearances are in need of adjustment, but it is advisable for all "Dominator" owners to check the clearances with a feeler gauge every 1,500 miles. An adjustment is then generally necessary.

**The Correct Valve Clearances.** For the 1955–8 engines of Models 88, 99 the recommended valve clearances are 0·002 in. for inlet valves and 0·003 in. for exhaust valves. The correct valve clearances for the engines fitted to 1959–63 Standard and de Luxe Norton Models 88, 99 are 0.003 in. and 0·005 in. for inlet and exhaust valves respectively. In the case of the 1962–3 Standard and de Luxe Model 650, the 1964–5 750 cc "Atlas," and all Sports Special (SS) models the clearances for the inlet and exhaust valves should be 0·006 in. and 0·008 in. respectively. Clearances of 0·006 in. and 0·008 in. are also recommended for the inlet and exhaust valves of engines fitted to 1955–63 Standard and De Luxe models when such machines are run on full throttle for prolonged periods. Note that the valve clearances of all 1955–65 engines should be checked with the engine *cold*.

**Checking and Adjusting Valve Clearances (All Engines).** Except on some 1955–8 engines the cams have quietening ramps and in order to make an accurate check and adjustment of each valve clearance the tappet concerned must contact the centre of the cam base-circle. The following procedure *must* be used for all 1958 and later engines. It is also convenient to use this method for earlier engines, although on these engines the clearance for each valve can be checked and if necessary adjusted after turning the engine so that the valve concerned is fully closed. The opening of the other inlet or exhaust valve can be disregarded.

*Inlet Valves.* Dealing first with the inlet valve clearances, remove the single nut and washer securing the rear (inlet) cover to the rocker-box, and withdraw the cover. Both inlet valves and rockers are then exposed as shown in Fig. 31. Now slowly rotate the engine until one valve is *just fully* open. With a suitable feeler gauge check the clearance between the stem of the other (closed) inlet valve and the adjuster on the rocker. The feeler gauge should just enter without any pressure being necessary.

If the valve clearance is found to be incorrect, with the small spanner provided in the tool kit hold the square end of the adjuster and loosen its lock-nut. Insert the correct size feeler gauge and turn the adjuster *clockwise* until the feeler is just pinched but able to move about fairly easily. Then while preventing the adjuster from moving, tighten the lock-nut and again check the valve clearance. Deal with the other inlet valve similarly. Slowly rotate the engine until the valve already dealt with is just fully open, and check and if necessary adjust the clearance for the second inlet valve. Finally replace and secure the rocker-box cover after checking that its joint washer is sound and correctly positioned.

*Exhaust Valves.* Having dealt with the inlet valve clearances, check and if necessary adjust the exhaust-valve clearances. Remove both front (exhaust) covers from the rocker-box after removing the four securing nuts and washers. Now rotate the engine slowly until one exhaust valve is *fully* open. Then check and if necessary adjust the clearance between the stem of the other (closed) exhaust valve and the adjuster on the rocker,

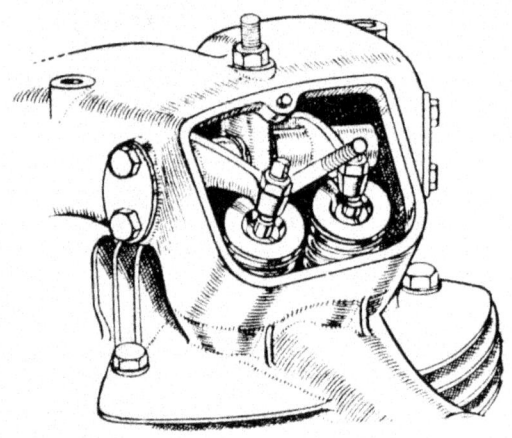

Fig. 31. Rear Cover Removed from Rocker-box Showing Rocker Arms with Adjusters for Inlet Valve Clearances

An independent housing (*see* Fig. 40) is provided for each exhaust-valve rocker and adjuster.

using the same procedure as previously described for the inlet valve. Further rotate the engine until the exhaust valve dealt with is *fully* open and check and if necessary adjust the clearance for the other exhaust valve. After tightening the lock-nut for each adjuster, again check the valve clearance. During its tightening the adjuster sometimes moves slightly. Finally replace and secure both rocker-box covers after making sure that their joint washers are sound and properly positioned.

## DECARBONIZING AND VALVE GRINDING

Decarbonizing, a top overhaul, should only be undertaken when symptoms develop which indicate that this is *necessary*. These symptoms which usually are noticeable after covering about 8,000 miles are: (*a*) a marked decline in the power output of the engine; (*b*) a tendency for the engine to run hotter than normal; (*c*) knocking under the slightest provocation; (*d*) a tendency for the sparking plugs to become dirty quickly; (*e*) lack of a crisp exhaust note. A top overhaul necessitates taking off the cylinder head and removing all carbon deposits from the piston crowns and the combustion chambers.

When the cylinder head is removed it is advisable also to remove the valves so that the ports in the cylinder head can be effectively cleaned, the valves and their seats inspected, and the valves if necessary ground-in. Cylinder block removal is quite unnecessary unless poor engine compression (not caused by faulty valves), piston slap or the emergence of blue smoke from the exhausts develop. Such symptoms indicate that a close examination of the pistons, piston rings and cylinder bores is desirable.

**Removing Petrol Tank (1955–9 Models 88, 99).** See that the petrol tap is turned off and disconnect the petrol pipe, using two spanners, one for holding the tap and the other for releasing the union nut. Remove the two wing nuts located centrally beneath the dual-seat and withdraw the dualseat. The bolt tensioning the tank steel securing-strap is thereby exposed. Remove this bolt, bend back the strap, and lift the tank off the rubber pads taped to the frame top tubes.

**Petrol Tank Removal (All 1960 Models Onwards).** Ensure that the petrol tap is in the off position. Disconnect the petrol pipe, using two spanners, one for the tap and one for the union nut. Release the single Dzus fastener at the rear of the dualseat and withdraw the latter rearwards from the two pegs on the frame at the front. These pegs support the dualseat with rubber bushes secured to its underside.

Free the single rubber band which secures the petrol tank at its rear, and unscrew the two inverted bolts positioned at its front. These bolts have rubber bushes above and below the frame lugs. The bushes above have a plain steel washer between them and the tank, while the bottom bushes are in steel cups. The bolts are shouldered so that when tightened fully the rubber bushes are not over compressed. Now withdraw the petrol tank.

**To Remove Cylinder Head (All Engines).** First remove the petrol tank as previously described. Next remove the Amal "monobloc" type carburettor, leaving it attached to the machine by the throttle, air cable. On some engines two carburettors are provided and both must be removed. Remove the exhaust pipe and silencer as a unit from each side of the motor-cycle. Disconnect the H.T. leads from both sparking plugs and also the engine steady-stay from the top of the rocker-box. Also disconnect the oil feed pipe to the overhead-rocker mechanism by unscrewing both banjo connexion-bolts positioned at the extreme top of the rocker-box. Be careful not to lose the fibre washers.

Remove the five hexagon-headed bolts visible above the cylinder head fins (*see* Fig. 38), the two nuts between the exhaust ports, and also the nut below the inlet ports and the nut from beneath each exhaust port. These three nuts are accessible through the cylinder-head fins. Now free and raise the cylinder head. If the joint between the cylinder block and the cylinder head is tight, free the head by directing a sharp tap below one exhaust port, using a mallet or a suitable block of wood. Do *not* use a hammer. When raising the cylinder head see that the gasket comes clean away with the head or remains in position on top of the cylinder block.

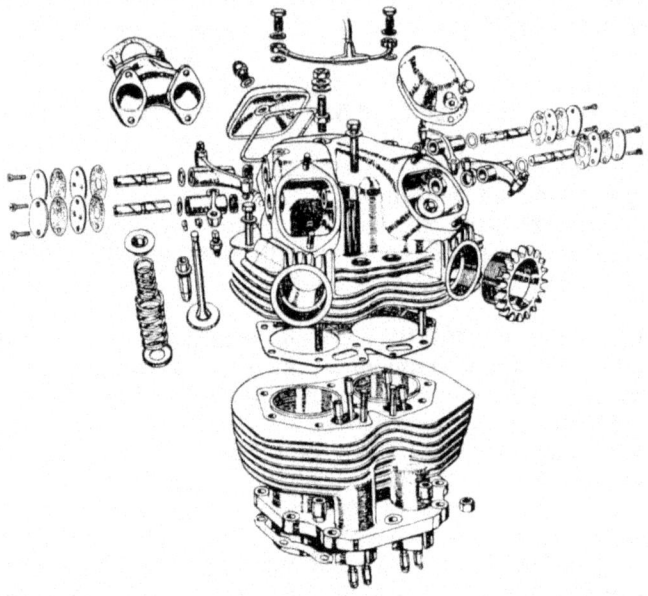

FIG. 32. EXPLODED VIEW OF UPPER PART OF NORTON "DOMINATOR" ENGINE SHOWING CYLINDER HEAD, CYLINDER BLOCK, ETC.
The general design is almost identical on all 1955–65 engines.

Raise the cylinder head as high as is practicable and obtain an assistant to feed the four push-rods into the head until they are clear of the cylinder block. Then tilt the cylinder head backwards and completely remove it.

**Removing Valves (All Engines).** As stated on page 69, valve removal is desirable for two reasons when decarbonizing. Their removal is easy after withdrawing the cylinder head. First expose the two inlet valves by removing the single upper cover from the rear of the rocker-box. The stud which secures the cover should also be removed. Remove the two upper covers from the front of the rocker-box so as to expose the two exhaust valves. Then remove each valve. Rotate its actuating rocker

## GENERAL MAINTENANCE

until it is sufficiently clear of the valve stem to enable a proprietary valve-spring compressor of the type shown in Fig. 33 to be used for compressing the duplex valve spring to enable the split collet to be removed. After this is done the duplex spring and the outer collar can be lifted off and the valve withdrawn from the combustion chamber.

Place each valve, together with its springs, outer collar, split collet, and heat-insulating washer (if removed) so that it cannot be disturbed and so

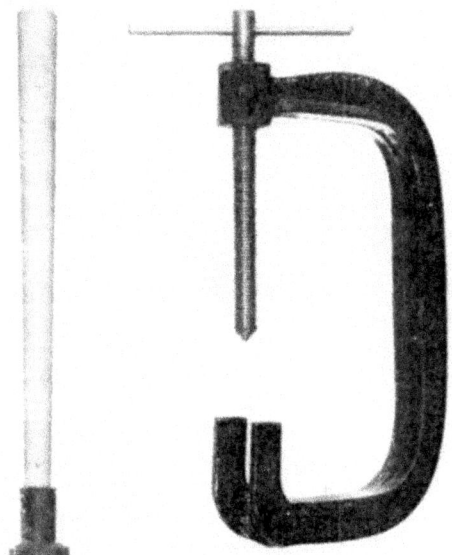

FIG. 33. TWO TYPICAL PROPRIETARY TOOLS FOR DEALING WITH THE VALVES

Above is shown a valve-spring compressor and below a suction-type tool for grinding-in the four valves.

that these components can be identified and subsequently replaced in their original positions. On no account interchange any of the inlet and exhaust valves. On later type engines the inlet valves have appreciably larger diameter heads than the exhaust valves and accidental interchanging of the valves is not so likely as on earlier engines.

**Decarbonizing Pistons and Cylinder Head.** This should be done thoroughly. Rotate the engine with the kick-starter until both pistons are at the top of their strokes and chip off all carbon deposits from the piston crowns with a proprietary scraper, the end of a six-inch steel rule, or a blunt screwdriver. Be extremely careful not to scratch or otherwise damage the comparatively soft aluminium-alloy surfaces, and on no account use an abrasive to polish them. When decarbonizing each piston it is advisable to rest an old piston ring on top of it. This will prevent a thin ridge of carbon from being removed between the top edge of the piston and the cylinder bore. The maintenance of good engine compression is thereby assisted.

Remove all traces of carbon from the cylinder-head combustion chambers. As in the case of aluminium-alloy pistons, care must be taken not to damage or scratch the combustion-chamber surfaces. Thoroughly clean the inlet and exhaust ports, and be specially careful not to allow the scraper to damage the valve seats. Do not forget to clean both sparking-plug holes.

**Inspecting the Valves.** Scrutinize closely the valve faces and also their seats in the cylinder head. The seats deteriorate more slowly than the valve faces. If any appreciable scaling or pitting is present, this indicates that the valves need grinding-in. Deep pitting (usually the result of running with insufficient valve clearances or an incorrect mixture), however, cannot be remedied by grinding-in, and it is usually necessary to have the valves refaced and the seats recut by a Norton repair specialist or by the Service Dept. of Norton Motors Ltd., Plumstead Road, London, S.E.18. The average Norton owner rarely has the necessary facilities to hand.

**The Valve Springs.** Unless the engine has been run at a very high temperature, the valve springs are unlikely to settle down unduly or collapse partially, especially as heat-resisting washers are interposed between the valve-spring inner collars and the cylinder head. Most valve springs, however, eventually weaken. It is a good plan occasionally to check their free length. The normal free length of the inner and outer valve springs is 1·53 in. and 1·70 in. respectively. If their free length is found to be $\frac{3}{16}$ in. or more below the normal just stated, it is desirable to fit *new* valve springs, assuming that you wish to obtain maximum r.p.m. from your engine.

**Grinding-in the Valves.** Before doing this remove all carbon from the valve heads and stems. Where the valve faces and seats are only slightly pitted it is generally satisfactory to use a *fine grade* valve grinding paste such as Richford's, but if pitting is fairly extensive, use a *medium grade* paste. A coarse grade paste should not be used unless the pitting is very extensive and, as has been mentioned in the previous paragraph, deeply pitted valve faces and seats cannot be satisfactorily rectified by grinding-in. If you renew one or more valves remember that initial grinding-in is necessary. Never grind-in a valve more than is absolutely necessary. An excessively ground-in valve becomes "pocketed" and loses its efficiency.

Before grinding-in a valve with the cylinder head on a table or bench, make sure that the valve and seat faces are quite clean. With the finger tip or a small piece of rag smear a *thin* film of grinding paste on the whole of the valve face and insert the valve in its guide. Be sure that it is the correct guide. If available, it is a good plan to insert a light spring under the valve head. This renders it unnecessary to lift the valve frequently off its seat by hand when periodically turning it to a new position to prevent the formation of rings or grooves.

Hold the valve with a suction-type tool (*see* Fig. 33) applied to its head, or a hand vice secured to its stem and, while maintaining an even pressure, rotate the valve backwards and forwards *about a quarter of a turn* in each direction, pausing every few oscillations to raise the valve from its seat to a new position. Cease grinding-in when the valve begins to "sing" and no "cut" can be felt. Then apply some more grinding paste to the valve face after cleaning both faces. Continue grinding-in until there is a perfectly smooth matt-ring round the face of the valve and seat, indicating that contact between them is perfect. About $\frac{1}{32}$ in. width of contact (slightly more for an exhaust valve) is quite sufficient. When you have completed grinding-in, thoroughly clean the faces of the valve and its seat with a paraffin- or petrol-soaked rag, being most careful to remove *all* traces of the grinding-in paste.

**Replacing the Valves (All Engines).** First see that all valves, valve seats, valve guides, collars, and ports are absolutely clean. Smear each valve stem with some clean engine oil before inserting the valve into the correct guide. Then replace the valve and fit the heat-resisting washer (where provided), the inner collar (if removed), the inner and outer valve springs, and the outer collar. With a proprietary valve-spring compressor (*see* Fig. 33) compress the duplex valve-spring and fit the split collet to the groove near the end of the valve stem. By applying a little thick grease to the groove or to the insides of the split-collet halves you will find that the collet sticks more readily in the groove until compression on the valve spring is released and the outer collar engages the collet. Make sure that the collet beds down properly into the collar. After replacing all four valves fit the stud for the rocker-box rear cover. This was removed to facilitate the removal of the inlet valves.

**To Remove Cylinder Block (All Engines).** Do not remove the cylinder block unless for some reason (*see* page 69) you wish to inspect the pistons, piston rings, and cylinder bores. Its removal is quite simple once you have removed the petrol tank and cylinder head as described on pages 69 to 70.

Before removing the cylinder block on 1955–7 models with dynamo-lighting equipment, first remove the dynamo. Disconnect its electrical leads, remove the three end-screws, slacken the dynamo securing strap, and withdraw the dynamo.

To withdraw the cylinder block, first rotate the engine until both pistons are at bottom-dead-centre and then remove the nine cylinder-block base nuts (seven large, and two small). To assist the removal of some of these nuts raise the cylinder block slightly. Now, standing astride the machine, slowly raise the cylinder block until the pistons emerge from the cylinder bores. When doing this avoid if possible damaging the paper joint-washer on the crankcase. It is desirable to have an assistant to steady the pistons as they clear the cylinder bores, and also to relieve you of the considerable weight of the cylinder block. Removing the cylinder block single-handed is liable to damage the pistons.

As soon as you are able to remove the cylinder block, cover the exposed opening in the crankcase with a clean duster to prevent the accidental entry of grit or foreign objects. If the paper washer for the crankcase and cylinder-block joint has become damaged, remove it and clean up the joint face. A very suitable implement is a carpenter's scraper plate.

**Removing the Pistons (All Engines).** Piston removal is not necessary unless their condition is such that they require renewal or unless loss of compression indicates that the piston rings require close examination and possible renewal. The two pistons which are *not* interchangeable each have two compression and one scraper ring. Remove each piston as described below.

First, with the opening in the crankcase completely covered, remove both gudgeon-pin circlips with a pair of sharp-nosed pliers. Discard these circlips as new ones must be fitted when replacing the piston. If the engine has become heavily carbonized, scrape off the carbon from the narrow land outside each circlip before attempting to extract the fully-floating gudgeon-pin.

The gudgeon-pin on some of the earlier engines can be pushed out by hand immediately the circlips have been removed. On most engines, however, it is a tight fit when the engine is cold and it is necessary to warm the piston to facilitate its removal. Wrap round it a cloth which has been immersed in boiling water and wrung out, or alternatively lay an electric iron on the piston crown. If no heating facilities are available, or if the gudgeon-pin is a tight fit even after warming the piston, press out the gudgeon-pin with a proprietary tool such as that shown in Fig. 34. Its method of use is self obvious.

After removing the gudgeon-pin make a nick on one end to ensure its being replaced in its original position. For the same reason mark the inside of the piston. Always handle both pistons with great care. Being made of light-alloy, they can easily be distorted or cracked.

**Piston Ring Condition.** Good engine compression is dependent on the condition of the piston rings as well as the state of the valves and cylinder-block bores. Each piston has two compression rings and one scraper ring.

On 650 cc engines the latter is a special "Twiflex" oil control ring. To function efficiently the piston rings must: (*a*) have ample springiness; (*b*) be bright and not discoloured over their entire external surfaces to indicate good contact with the cylinder bores; (*c*) be quite free in the piston grooves but not have excessive side clearance; (*d*) have the correct gap

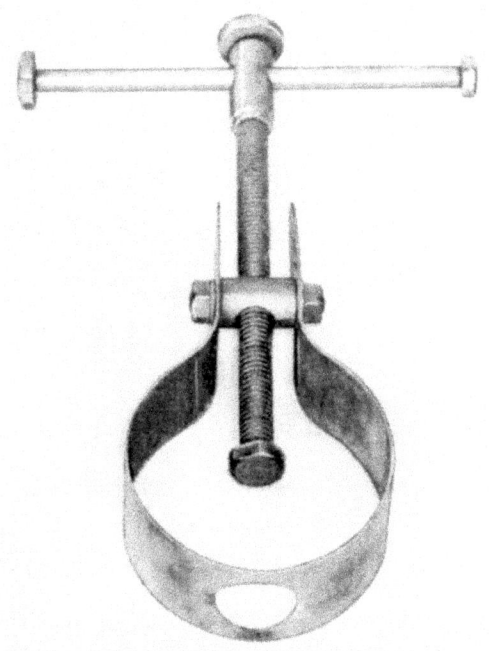

FIG. 34. A USEFUL PROPRIETARY TOOL FOR REMOVING AND FITTING TIGHT GUDGEON-PINS

This tool has three different size pressure-pads to fit varying sizes of gudgeon-pin.

between their ends when in the cylinder bores; and (*e*) be inserted in the cylinder bores with their gaps spaced at 120 degrees to each other.

Renew piston rings which are dull or stained through lack of proper contact with the cylinder bores, also rings which have lost good springiness and have a gap between their ends (when in the cylinder bores) exceeding 0·028 in.–0·030 in. Also renew rings which are vertically loose in their grooves or are scored. Stuck piston rings which cease to function satisfactorily can often be made to operate properly after cleaning the piston grooves with paraffin and a suitable scraper. A convenient tool for removing carbon deposits is a piece of old piston ring ground at one end like a chisel. However, generally speaking, it is unwise to remove carbon deposits from the base of the ring grooves and the backs of the rings unless new rings are to be fitted.

When fitting new rings remove all carbon deposits from the bases of the piston grooves, and from their sides, otherwise the side clearances and gaps of the new rings are likely to be insufficient. The correct side clearance on all 1955 and later engines is 0·0015 in.–0·0035 in. Before fitting a new ring check its gap by inserting it squarely (by means of the piston) in the least worn part of the cylinder bore (about ½ in. from the

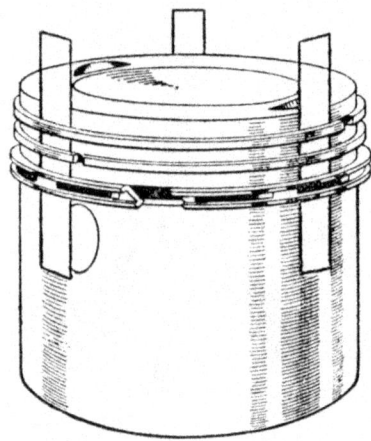

FIG. 35. THE SAFEST METHOD OF REMOVING AND FITTING PISTON RINGS

bottom) and measuring the gap with a feeler gauge. The gap for compression and scraper rings should be 0·008 in.–0·010 in. If the gap is insufficient, clamp the ring between two wood blocks in a vice and then carefully file one of its diagonal ends as required. A final word of advice. Always use piston rings supplied by Norton Motors Ltd., and do not attempt to fit oversize rings.

**Removing and Fitting Piston Rings.** Piston rings are made of cast-iron and are of very small section. They must therefore always be handled with great care to avoid breaking them. Do not open them out wider than is required to slip them on or off a piston. Used rings should be kept in their original positions and the same way up. New chromium-plated compression rings are reversible unless marked "TOP". The second compression ring when new is taper-faced and should be fitted with the mark "TOP" uppermost. New scraper rings are reversible.

The safest method of removing and fitting piston rings is to insert three small strips of thin sheet-metal (about ½ in. wide and 2 in. long) under the rings as shown in Fig. 35 and then gently ease the rings off or on individually. Fitting a special "Twiflex" oil-control ring (*see* Fig. 36) on a 650 cc engine requires a special procedure (see below).

**Fitting "Twiflex" Oil-control Ring (650 cc Engines).** The following is the correct procedure.

1. Check that the ring groove and oil drain holes are quite clean and

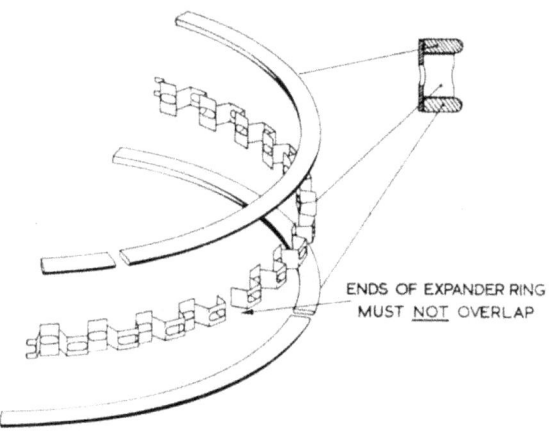

FIG. 36. SHOWING DETAILS OF SPECIAL "TWIFLEX" OIL CONTROL RING FITTED TO PISTONS OF 650 CC ENGINES

This unusual type of scraper ring comprises two thin rings (called rails) located on each side of the stepped portion of an expander ring. It is essential that the ends of the expander ring meet each other without overlapping when each piston is being inserted into the cylinder block.

then wind a rail (a thin ring) on to the piston skirt just below the oil-control ring groove.

2. Place the expander ring in the groove with its ends butted and in line with the pin hole. Take special care to see that the ends of the expander ring do not overlap. They must butt.

3. Slip the ends of the rail on the piston skirt into the groove beside the expander ring. The rail gap should be one inch to the left of the butted ends of the expander ring.

4. At this stage do not push the back of the expander ring into the piston groove. Wind the other rail down over the lands into the scraper groove on the upper side of the expander with the gap one inch to the right of the butted ends of the expander ring.

5. With the thumb-nail work the back of the expander ring down into the groove between the rails. Centralize the ring on the assembly but do not move the assembly more than is required.

6. The oil-control ring will now be complete in its groove with the rails supported on the expander ring lugs. It may seem rather stiff to move, but ignore this.

**Replacing the Pistons (All Engines).** The "Dominator" pistons are *not* interchangeable and this is indicated by the angular position of the recesses provided in their crowns to enable the valve heads to clear them. Should it be necessary to fit a new piston for any reason, make sure that you obtain a near-side or off-side piston as required. New pistons can be fitted either way round, but after use each piston should always be fitted in its original position as follows.

It is assumed that the piston rings if removed have been correctly replaced (*see* page 76). Fit a new circlip to the piston to be fitted, using a pair of sharp-nosed pliers, and offer up the piston the correct way round, to the small-end of the connecting-rod. Then oil and (after warming the piston if necessary) insert the gudgeon-pin, pressing it right home against the circlip already fitted by means of a proprietary tool such as that shown in Fig. 34, assuming that the gudgeon-pin is a tight fit. Afterwards fit a new circlip on the other side of the gudgeon-pin. Check that both circlips are properly bedded down in the piston-boss grooves, and that when you have fitted both pistons the forward recesses for the valves in their crowns are farther apart than those at the rear of the engine.

**To Replace the Cylinder Block (All Engines).** Clean thoroughly the joint face of the cylinder block and the crankcase face on which it fits. Renew the paper washer unless this is in perfect condition. Smear the cylinder block face lightly with some jointing compound, stick the washer to it, and make sure that its oil return hole is unobstructed. Liberally smear some clean engine oil over both pistons and also over the cylinder bores. Space the six piston rings so that their gaps are at 120 degrees to each other and position the pistons so that they are at or near bottom-dead-centre. Then, preferably with some assistance, replace the cylinder block. Fitting the cylinder block single-handed is risky.

Before attempting to fit the cylinder block, however, first fit piston-ring compressors (obtainable from Norton spares stockists or from the Norton Service Dept.) over both pistons. All the rings and ring gaps should be covered and about $\frac{1}{8}$ in. of piston should remain visible above each compressor. It is desirable to lay two (dead straight) steel rods, e.g. tommy-bars, from a spanner set, beneath the pistons across the crankcase top face, one at the front and one at the rear. Be careful not to incline the rods by resting them on the timing cover. This arrangement ensures that the pistons are held quite square and steady during the lowering of the cylinder block.

Lower the cylinder block gently over the two pistons, forcing the piston-ring compressors down until they emerge from the bottom of the piston

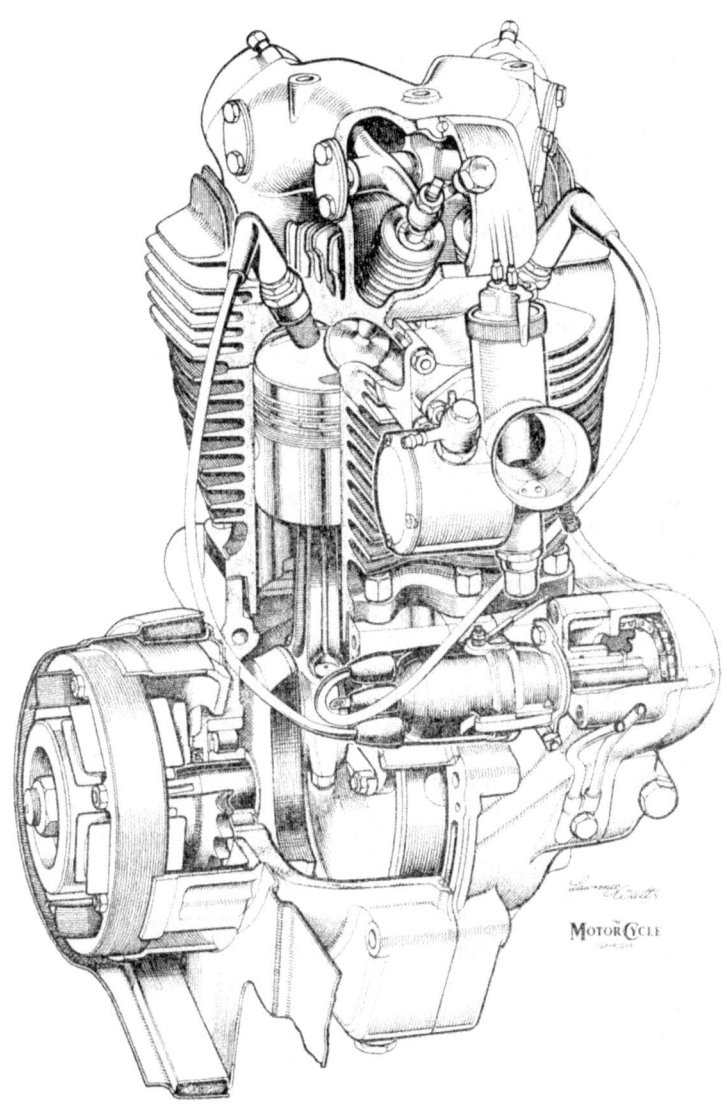

Fig. 37. Cut-away View of 600 cc Norton "Dominator" Engine with Coil Ignition

The engine shown is that for the 1958 Model 99. An alternator charges the battery for lighting and ignition. Coil ignition is also provided on all other 1958 and later engines except Sports Special engines which have a magneto fitted in place of the contact breaker-distributor unit shown. Earlier engines have a dynamo fitted as well as a magneto.

(*By courtesy of "Motor Cycle," London*)

skirts. Remove both compressors and the steel rods (if used), lower the cylinder block to within about ¼ in. of the crankcase face, and replace the nine cylinder base securing-nuts. Then lower the cylinder block completely and just pinch down the two nuts on either side of the block, tightening them in a diagonal order. Tighten the three remaining large nuts, and finally the two $\tfrac{9}{16}$ in. nuts at the front of the block. On a 1955–7 model replace the dynamo, tightening the end screws before tightening the securing strap.

**Fitting the Cylinder Head (All Engines).** If the cylinder-head gasket is not in perfect condition, renew it. If you use the same gasket, fit it to the cylinder block with the same face uppermost as hitherto. Rotate the engine until both pistons are at top-dead-centre and place the cylinder head on top of the cylinder block. Then tilt it backwards and insert the four push-rods into the two cylinder-head tunnels. The inlet push-rods are appreciably longer than the exhaust push-rods (*see* Fig. 32) and one of each must be inserted into each cylinder-head tunnel, with the inlet (longer) rods nearer the centre.

Gently lower the cylinder-head and as it approaches its normal position, allow the four push-rods to engage their respective tappets. When the cylinder head is within about ¼ in. of the gasket on the cylinder block, support it in this position with two short sleeve nuts taken from beneath the exhaust ports. Place this temporary packing between the cylinder-block top fin and the cylinder-head bottom fin and engage the ball ends of the overhead rockers with the upper ends of the push-rods. Each inlet push-rod can be drawn into position by means of a piece of bent wire, access being obtained through the exhaust inspection apertures. Then remove the temporary packing and fully lower the cylinder head on to the gasket. Make sure that the inlet and exhaust overhead rockers do properly engage the push-rods.

Replace all ten nuts and bolts which secure the cylinder head. Tighten them down lightly first and then firmly in the order shown in Fig. 38. Finally re-connect the oil feed pipe to the overhead rocker mechanism, the engine steady stay, and the H.T. leads to the two sparking plugs. Also replace the carburettor or carburettors and each silencer and exhaust pipe unit. Adjust the valve clearances as required (*see* page 67).

**Replacing Petrol Tank (1955–9 Models 88, 99).** If you fit new rubber pads to the frame top-tubes be sure that they are well bedded down and securely taped so that there is no risk of metal-to-metal contact occurring between the petrol tank and the frame. Pull the tank-securing strap into position, fit the bolt and nut, and tighten the latter sufficiently to prevent any loosening by vibration. Be careful not to over-stress the tank structure by excessive tightening. Re-connect the petrol pipe, using

## GENERAL MAINTENANCE

one spanner to hold the tap and another to tighten the union nut. Finally replace the dualseat.

**Replacing Petrol Tank (All 1960 Models Onwards).** Verify that the two rubber pads on which the tank rests at the rear, and which are taped to the frame tubes, are positioned so that the tank does not make metal contact with the frame. Replace the two bolts with their cups, rubbers, and washers at the front, and pull the rubber band over the hook at the rear. Re-connect the petrol pipe and be careful not to over-tighten the

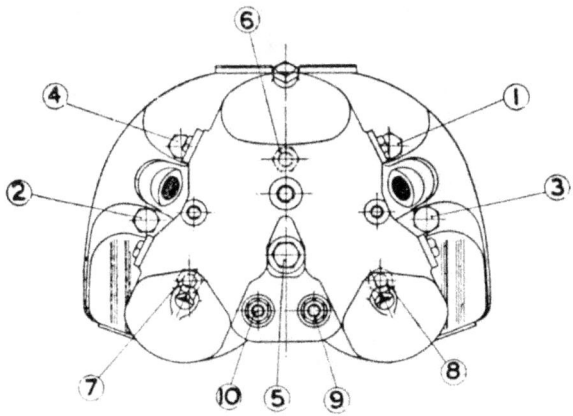

FIG. 38. THE CORRECT ORDER FOR TIGHTENING AND LOOSENING THE TEN NUTS AND BOLTS WHICH SECURE THE CYLINDER HEAD

union nut, otherwise the tap may unscrew when the pipe is next disconnected. Replace the dualseat.

### MISCELLANEOUS ENGINE OVERHAUL

**Removing Overhead Rockers, Spindles (1955-65).** It is advisable first to heat the cylinder head to at least the temperature of boiling water. It is assumed that the inlet and exhaust valves have already been removed (*see* page 70). Remove the pairs of screws which secure the oval cover-plates to the sides of the rocker-box.

On all 1955-65 engines the oval cover-plates secured to the sides of the rocker-box are entirely separate from the rocker spindles (*see* Fig. 40) and two oval plates and two washers are fitted over each rocker-spindle hole. The inner plate has two projections for locating the radial position of the spindle and the latter has a threaded hole at its outer end. To withdraw the inlet rocker spindle, use a $\frac{5}{16}$ in. × 26 thread bolt (taken from some part of the motor-cycle) as an extractor after interposing a piece of tube or a large nut between the bolt and cylinder head.

Note that the rocker hub has a spring washer at one end and a plain thrust washer at the other end. Remove these carefully before extracting each inlet rocker, or allow to fall away when removing the rocker. After

Fig. 39. Showing Some Details of a Model 88SS "Dominator" Norton with its Engine Assembled after Decarbonizing

1. Recommended oil level in tank.
2. Oil tank drain plug.
3. Oil pipe leading to rocker-box.
4. Oil return pipe to tank.
5. Oil feed pipe to engine.
6. Gearbox filler-orifice cover.
7. Clutch-cable adjuster.
8. Gearbox oil-level plug.
9. Gear indicator.
10. H.T. cables from magneto.
11. Engine r.p.m. indicator-drive gearbox.

removing an inlet rocker until its hub is clear of the spindle hole bosses, it is necessary to turn it upside down in order to remove it completely.

The exhaust rockers can be removed similarly to the inlet rockers, but it is not necessary to invert each rocker in order to remove it.

**Fitting Overhead Rockers, Spindles (1955–65 Engines).** When fitting new or used inlet and exhaust rockers and spindles, reverse the dismantling procedure. It is desirable first to heat the cylinder head in boiling water. Place each rocker in position, adding the plain thrust-washer to the outer end of the hub and maintaining an end load on the rocker while inserting the spring washer. The end load put on the spring washer will hold the

GENERAL MAINTENANCE 83

assembly in position while inserting the spindle. The rocker spindles have a "flat" on one side. All "flats" must face *inwards* towards the centre of the engine, and the slot across the spindle must lie *horizontal*. See that the oil hole in each spindle mates up with the oil-feed hole in the rocker-box.

After fitting an inlet or exhaust rocker-spindle, fit a paper washer to the oval face on the side of the rocker-box after smearing it with some oil; fit the oval plate with its tags engaging the spindle slot; fit another paper

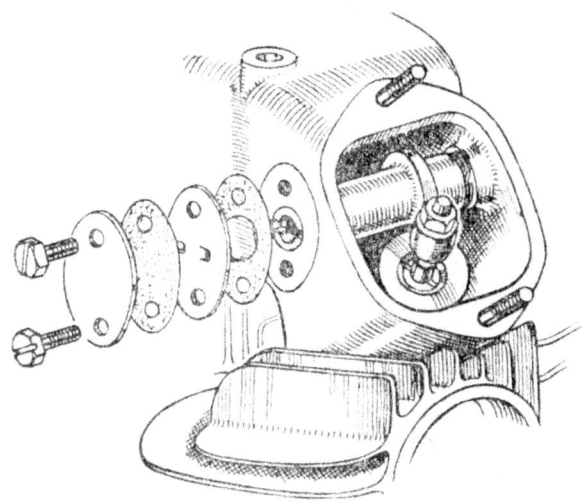

FIG. 40. OVAL COVER-PLATES, WASHERS AND SECURING SCREWS REMOVED FROM SIDE OF ROCKER-BOX FOR ROCKER SPINDLE REMOVAL

washer; fit the plain oval-plate; finally secure the assembly by fitting and tightening the two securing screws (*see* Fig. 40).

**Removing and Fitting Tappets (All Engines).** It is highly improbable that the tappets will need any attention until a very big mileage has been covered. They are fitted inside the cylinder block and are readily accessible when the block is removed.

Invert the cylinder block, remove the wire securing the tappet division-plate screws and remove the screws. Then push out the tappets and the division plate. If tight, a light blow directed on the opposite end of the tappets will effectively free the plate.

Do not interchange the tappets either singly or in pairs, and do not fit them the opposite way round. Assembling is quite straightforward, but do not forget to wire the division-plate screws. If the tappets are correctly fitted, their bevelled edges are together and to the front of the engine.

**The Valve Guides (All Engines).** The inlet and exhaust valve guides are a driving fit in the cylinder head which must be heated to at least the boiling point of water to enable the guides to be removed and new ones fitted. Removal and fitting should be done with a double-diameter drift of mild steel 6 in.–8 in. long. Its smaller diameter should be an accurate fit in the bore of the guide and its outside diameter should be fractionally less than the outside diameter of the valve guide. The shoulder should, of course, be turned square and the pilot or small diameter part should be almost as long as the valve guide itself. Valve seats must be trued up with a cutter after fitting new guides to ensure that the guides and the seats are in true alignment.

**To Remove and Fit Timing Cover (All Engines).** Do not disturb the oil feed and return pipes, which are soldered into a junction block secured to the *crankcase*. Remove the 12 cheese-headed screws which secure the cover and withdraw it. If tight, lever gently behind the pressure-release valve boss, and tap lightly with a wooden mallet on the opposite side of the cover. Be careful not to lose the small rubber washer which comprises an oil seal between the oil pump and the timing cover.

When replacing the timing cover, see that both joint faces are clean and smear them with some jointing compound such as "Wellseal" which is non-hardening. Fit a new paper washer if this is not in perfect condition. Verify that the oil pump rubber sealing-washer is in position. Be careful not to damage the oil-seal when entering the engine mainshaft into the timing cover. If there appears to be any obstruction, do not press the cover right home. Replace all 12 cheese-headed screws, checking that there is an aluminium or fibre washer under each head, and lightly tighten each screw before finally tightening each pair of opposite screws.

**Oil Pump Removal and Fitting.** The oil pump rarely gives any trouble. When the timing cover is removed it is a simple matter to remove the oil pump if necessary.

**The Oil Pump Seal.** This must always exert some pressure against the timing cover. Note the advice given on page 18.

**Removing Timing Sprockets and Chains (1955–7 Engines).** On 1955–7 "Dominators" with dynamo lighting and magneto ignition the following is the recommended procedure. First remove the timing cover as previously described. Then withdraw the whole sprocket assembly with the chains in position. This necessitates removing the timing-chain tensioner which is secured to a boss in the timing chest by two nuts.

Remove the nut securing the camshaft sprocket and also the pin holding the automatic ignition-advance mechanism to the magneto spindle. As the pin is removed the latter is automatically withdrawn. The camshaft sprocket, however, may need the application of a standard type of sprocket extractor. The intermediate gear and sprocket will, of course, readily come away from the spindle. Remove the oil pump worm (left-hand thread) and withdraw the half-time pinion with a special extractor obtainable for this purpose.

**Fitting Timing Sprockets and Chains (1955–7 Engines).** On models with dynamo lighting and magneto ignition, first fit the oil-retaining disc and the triangular washer to the engine mainshaft. Then fit the pinion key. Also fit the half-time pinion with its chamfered edge outside and tap it home with a tubular drift.

Next fit the steel washer to the intermediate shaft, camshaft. The camshaft is the thicker of the two shafts. Now turn the engine until the marked tooth on the half-time pinion is in the top-dead-centre position. Smear some grease on both faces of the fibre gear which drives the dynamo. Position the gear on the flange of the sprocket, and to the other face of the gear fit the steel friction-washer locating it on the peg protruding from the sprocket flange. The previous application of grease will hold it.

Rotate the camshaft until its keyway is in the top-dead-centre position. Fit the magneto chain (the narrower one) on the inner of the two sprockets on the intermediate gear, and the camshaft chain on the other one. Rotate the intermediate gear until the marked gear tooth is in the bottom-dead-centre position. This will give a marked sprocket tooth in the topmost position. The camshaft sprocket also has a marked tooth which should also be in the top position when the sprocket is meshed with the chain. Now place the chain and sprocket assembly loosely in position, mesh the magneto sprocket and automatic ignition-advance mechanism with its driving chain, and push the whole assembly home.

On the dynamo-drive side the peg in the driving clutch sees that the back plate rotates with the front one on the sprocket, the fibre gear being in between. Verify carefully that all marked teeth are correctly positioned. When the marked pinion and gear teeth are correctly positioned and in mesh, both marked sprocket teeth should be in the top-dead-centre position, the intermediate-sprocket tooth having just entered the chain and the camshaft-sprocket tooth being just about to leave the chain. Replace and tighten the oil-pump worm and camshaft-sprocket nut, but do not replace the timing cover until you have retimed the magneto.

Fit the chain tensioner after the chain is positioned. Adjust its tension so that there is about $\frac{1}{8}$ in. whip in the top run of the chain.

**Removing Timing Sprockets and Chains (1958–65 Engines).** All engines except on Sports Special (SS) and 750 cc "Atlas" models have coil ignition. The SS and "Atlas" models have magneto ignition. The following instructions apply to the standard models having Lucas contact-breaker distributor units.

It is desirable to have the use of a cut-away dummy timing cover for supporting the intermediate gear spindle while the camshaft nut is slackened for dismantling, and for tightening it on assembly. It has a right-hand thread. Both chains are endless and it is therefore necessary to withdraw the whole sprocket assembly with the chains in position. Before doing this, however, remove the camshaft chain-tension slipper and its clamping plates, unscrew the camshaft nut, unscrew the oil pump driving-worm (left-hand thread), and remove the driving pin from the distributor spindle.

Be careful when removing and fitting the distributor spindle driving-pin. Use a $\frac{1}{8}$ in. parallel-pin punch and as the pin is driven out support the sprocket boss with a suitable weight from the opposite side. It is permissible to use the pin again, but renew it if there is any doubt about the way it fits when it is replaced and re-riveted. When riveting it, a weight such as a second hammer-head should be held against one end of the pin while the other is being turned over. The removal of the camshaft sprocket requires the use of a standard type sprocket puller. It is on a parallel shaft and not on a taper. A hardened steel washer is fitted on the intermediate gear spindle between the gear and the crankcase.

**Fitting Timing Sprockets and Chains (1958–65 Engines).** On the coil-ignition engines assemble as follows. Fit the oil-retaining disc (flange to outside), the triangular washer to the mainshaft, and the half-time pinion key. Fit the half-time pinion with its chamfered edge outside and tap it home with a tubular drift. Fit a hardened-steel washer to the intermediate shaft and fit the camshaft key. Rotate the engine until the marked tooth on the half-time pinion is at T.D.C. Rotate the camshaft until the keyway is also approximately at T.D.C.

Place the distributor chain (the narrower chain) on the inner of the two sprockets on the intermediate gear and the camshaft chain on the other one. Rotate the gear until the marked space between the teeth is at B.D.C. The chains when fitted obscure this mark. Therefore mark the tooth on either side of it with crayon or pencil. It will facilitate checking that it is correctly meshed with the crankshaft pinion.

This will provide a marked sprocket tooth in the 11 o'clock position. The camshaft sprocket also has a marked tooth which should be at 11 o'clock when the chain is fitted to both sprockets. Six outer plates on the camshaft chain should separate these marked teeth (*see* Fig. 41).

When the chain sprockets and gears are correctly meshed, push them home on their shafts, fit the camshaft nut, the oil pump driving-worm, and the chain-tension slipper parts. The thinner of the two clamping plates goes on first with its long end down, followed by the tensioner and the thicker plate with its long end up. Fit the fan-disc washers and nuts, and tighten the nuts lightly. Set the camshaft chain-tension so that there is $\frac{3}{16}$ in. minimum up-and-down movement in the centre of the chain run at its tightest point. Tighten the tensioner nuts and re-check. Do not adjust this chain too tight. While doing this, push the distributor sprocket over the driving spindle after making sure that the copper washer and tubular-steel spacer are already on the spindle. Remove the distributor cap and place a finger on the rotor while the sprocket is pushed home.

Unlike the camshaft sprocket, it is possible to get the distributor sprocket clear of its spindle and re-mesh it with the chain if necessary without disturbing the intermediate gear. Fit a dummy timing cover and tighten the camshaft nut and the oil pump driving-worm (left-hand thread).

On magneto-ignition SS and "Atlas" models mesh the automatic ignition-advance mechanism and driving sprocket with its driving chain

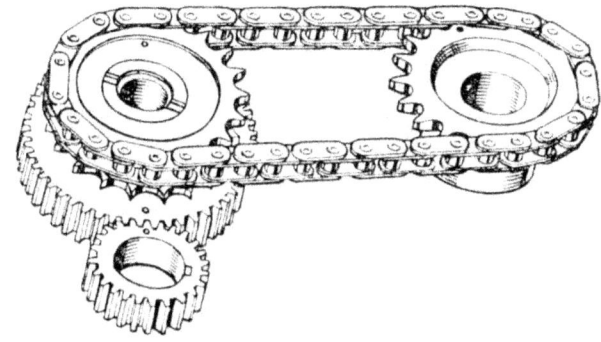

FIG. 41. THE CAMSHAFT CHAIN CORRECTLY POSITIONED ON THE SPROCKETS (1958–65 ENGINES)

at the same time as the camshaft chain and sprocket assembly is pushed on to its shafts. It should be entered on the magneto armature-spindle and the securing nut started a few threads prior to ignition timing.

**Timing Ignition (All 1958–63 Coil-ignition Engines).** First make sure that the distributor driving-chain has $\frac{3}{16}$ in. up-and-down movement of one run at its tightest point. The ignition timing will be upset by a slack chain. Make the required adjustment by slackening the two Allen nuts near the upper edge of the distributor adaptor. Gentle leverage or a tap with a mallet will pivot the assembly about the bottom stud enough to allow for normal chain adjustment. Adjust the gap between the contact-breaker contacts when wide open to be 0·015 in. Check the gap with a feeler gauge.

Remove both sparking plugs and rotate the engine until the marked tooth on the camshaft sprocket is at top centre position. This will bring the pistons to T.D.C. with *the near-side piston at the top of its compression stroke.* By inserting a thin metal rod as vertically as possible through the sparking plug hole, the exact T.D.C. position of the near-side piston can be felt and marked on the rod. Alternatively use a proprietary T.D.C. indicator. If a degree disc is fitted to the crankshaft for subsequently determining piston movement in degrees of crankshaft rotation, mark the point on its circumference which coincides with the pointer when the piston is at true T.D.C. When timing the ignition it is absolutely essential to place the near-side piston exactly at T.D.C. and not approximately at T.D.C.

Now turn the distributor until the brass contact of its rotor points directly *downwards*. Then note if the driving-pin holes in the sprocket

TABLE II

IGNITION TIMINGS FOR 1955–65 NORTON ENGINES

(On all engines the timings given apply to the near-side piston on its compression stroke with the ignition fully advanced)

| Norton Engine | CC | The Correct Timing |
|---|---|---|
| 1955–63 Model 88. | 497 | $\frac{1}{4}$ in. or 30° before T.D.C. |
| 1962–5 Model 88SS | 497 | $\frac{1}{4}$ in. or 30° before T.D.C. |
| 1956–62 Model 99. | 597 | 7·8 mm or 32° before T.D.C. |
| 1962 Model 99SS. | 597 | 7·8 mm or 32° before T.D.C. |
| 1962–3 Model 650 | 646 | 8·69 mm or 32° before T.D.C. |
| 1962–5 Model 650SS | 646 | 8·69 mm or 32° before T.D.C. |
| 1964–5 "Atlas" | 745 | 8·69 mm or 32° before T.D.C. |

and spindle line up. If they do not, ease the sprocket off the spindle and re-mesh it with the chain to the nearest tooth, push back on the spindle, and fit the driving pin as described on page 86.

Rotate the engine *backwards* until the *near-side piston* moves downwards the required distance before T.D.C. on its compression stroke, or the crankshaft degree disc (if fitted) indicates that the crankshaft has rotated backwards the required number of degrees, to the point when the contact-breaker contacts should begin to open. The correct ignition timings for all 1955–65 engines are given in the table shown above. These ignition timings should never be altered. When moving the piston to the correct position before T.D.C. on the compression stroke it is preferable and more accurate to use a degree disc to measure degrees of crankshaft rotation rather than to use a thin rod inserted through the plug hole to measure piston movement in fractions of an inch. However, either method can safely be used for ignition timing.

After positioning the piston in the correct position according to the table shown above, make sure that the piston does not move. Then slacken the pinch-bolt on the distributor clamp (it has a captive nut) and, while turning the rotor *clockwise* to the *fully advanced* position, slowly rotate the distributor body until the contact-breaker contacts just separate. To determine initial separation, insert a thin slip of cigarette-paper or celophane between the contacts and pull the slip gently. When it is just released the ignition timing is correct. Finally tighten the pinch-bolt on the distributor clamp and again check the ignition timing.

**Timing Ignition (All 1955-7, 1962-5 Magneto-ignition Engines).** Before timing the magneto first check that the contact-breaker gap is 0·012 in. plus or minus 0·001 in. with the contacts wide open (*see* page 64). Check on both cams.

Screw up the nut which secures the automatic ignition-advance mechanism to the armature shaft and check the magneto chain tension. It should have about $\frac{3}{16}$ in. whip midway between the sprockets at its tightest point. The magneto is flange-mounted on three waisted studs which permit of chain adjustment when loosened. Slacken the nut and continue to unscrew it until it just pulls the automatic ignition-advance mechanism off the taper.*

To obtain the correct ignition timing (*see* table on page 88) position the piston in the *near-side cylinder* the correct distance before T.D.C. on the *compression stroke*, measuring this distance with a thin metal rod inserted through the sparking plug hole or by crankshaft rotation measured with a crankshaft degree disc. Both methods have been previously referred to on page 88 in the section dealing with the timing of coil-ignition engines. When the piston has been correctly positioned deal with the contact-breaker. Its contacts must just open. Note that the *rear* H.T. lead from the magneto is attached to the *near-side* sparking plug, and that the Lucas magneto fires this plug when the contact-breaker rocker heel strikes the *bottom* cam.

With a small nut or wooden wedge prop the automatic ignition-advance mechanism *fully advanced*. Rotate the contact-breaker with the fingers so that a thin strip of cigarette paper or cellophane can just be withdrawn from between the points. Hold the contact-breaker still and with another hand screw up the centre nut on the automatic ignition-advance mechanism. Remove the wedge holding it advanced and tighten the nut, preferably with a ring spanner. Replace the wedge and again check the ignition timing. Do not forget to remove the wedge before replacing the timing cover.

---

* A few Model 88 Sports Specials (about 200) have an ignition lever on the handlebars used in conjunction with a plain driving-sprocket which fits on a taper exactly as where automatic ignition-advance mechanism is provided. The ignition timing procedure is the same whether or not an ignition lever is fitted, but in the latter case the lever must be moved to the *fully advanced* position.

**Do Not Meddle With the Valve Timing.** The valve timing decided upon by the engine manufacturers is most suited for all normal riding and should not be interfered with. Provided that the timing sprockets and chains are fitted as described on pages 85 and 86, the valve timing will remain correct.

**To Remove Engine from "Featherbed" Frame (All 1955–65 Models Except Models 7, 77).** The engine and gearbox assembly is designed to be removed from the "featherbed" type frame *as a unit*. This also facilitates cleaning. To facilitate removal of the unit it is advisable to support the frame cradle on a wooden block or box.

First remove the petrol tank (*see* page 69), both exhaust pipes and silencers, the oil-bath chain case, the oil tank and the battery, together with their platform. Also remove the engine steady and disconnect all cables and electric wiring likely to prevent the engine and gearbox assembly being removed after releasing all attachments.

Remove the remaining bolts which secure the engine and gearbox assembly to the frame and lift the assembly clear of it. Probably it will be necessary to obtain some assistance to steady the motor-cycle during the withdrawal of the engine and gearbox unit. You should find no difficulty in subsequently separating the engine and gearbox.

**Major Engine Overhaul.** After a *very* considerable mileage has been covered wear of the big-end bearings and of the crankshaft main bearings will be indicated by noise coming from the crankcase, especially when the engine is under load. Worn big-end bearings cause a thumping noise and closing the throttle does not eliminate it. A rather similar noise is caused by wear of the crankshaft main bearings. If a tapping noise develops, this indicates that the small-end bushes are also worn. When the engine becomes noisy and power output also declines considerably it is desirable to submit the crankshaft assembly and crankcase to a thorough inspection and overhaul. All bearings which are found to be considerably worn should be renewed. A major overhaul of this nature requires considerable skill, some special tools, and preferably a workshop bench. Few motor-cyclists have the time, facilities or skill to tackle major engine overhaul and it is generally wise to entrust this work to a Norton repair specialist.

If you have good facilities available and feel able to tackle major engine overhaul yourself, the author would refer you to the technical instructions given in the official Maintenance Manual and Instruction Book applicable to your own particular machine, and to the Twin Cylinder Manual which covers the servicing of 1960 and later lightweight and heavyweight twin-cylinder Nortons. This manual is obtainable from Norton Motors, Ltd. or from one of their dealers or spares stockists. It includes useful tabulated

# GENERAL MAINTENANCE

technical data with dimensions and tolerances. Space at the author's disposal does not permit of major overhaul of the various types of engines dealt with in this handbook being included.

## CARE OF CHAINS

**Chain Lubrication.** The primary and secondary chains are subjected to severe stresses while transmitting power from the engine to the rear wheel. Adequate chain lubrication is therefore of vital importance and appropriate instructions are given on pages 25–6.

**Primary Chain Tension.** On all 1955–65 models the primary chain is enclosed in an oil-bath chain case. It is therefore well protected and, if the oil-bath chain case is regularly topped-up (*see* page 25), efficiently lubricated. Stretching occurs appreciably more slowly than is the case with a secondary chain except where the latter is provided with a chain case giving full enclosure. However, it is advisable to check the tension of the primary chain about every 2,000 miles. Remove the inspection cover from the oil-bath chain case (*see* Fig. 11) and check the tension of the chain midway between the sprockets. With the chain in its tightest position it should be possible to move the chain up and down with the fingers a total distance of $\frac{1}{2}$ in. to $\frac{3}{4}$ in. Where the deflexion exceeds $\frac{3}{4}$ in. an immediate adjustment should be made by moving the gearbox as described below.

**Primary Chain Adjustment (1955–6 Models).** Slacken the two bolts which secure the top and bottom of the Burman gearbox. Then tighten the primary chain until its tension is correct by turning the adjuster on the off-side of the machine *clockwise* as required. Afterwards firmly retighten the two gearbox securing-bolts and re-tension the secondary chain. Tightening the primary chain inevitably slackens the secondary chain because the two sprockets on which it runs become closer to each other.

**Primary Chain Adjustment (1956–65 Models).** An A.M.C. gearbox is fitted to some 1956 and all 1957–65 models. It pivots on its lower mounting bolt, and elongated holes are provided in the mounting plates for the top bolt so that the gearbox can be moved backwards or forwards as required to adjust the tension of the primary chain. A drawbolt fitted to the gearbox top bolt has a $\frac{3}{16}$ in. Whit. hexagon nut on either side of a stop riveted to the off-side mounting plate.

To tighten the primary chain, remove the oil-bath chain case inspection cover shown at (1) in Fig. 11, slacken the forward drawbolt nut and run it back with the fingers one or two threads. Slacken the gearbox top bolt ($\frac{7}{16}$ in. Whit. hex.) and slacken only slightly the gearbox bottom bolt ($\frac{3}{8}$ in. Whit. hex.). With a spanner applied to the rear drawbolt-nut, pull the gearbox backwards until the chain is tight. Now loosen the rear nut a few turns and tighten the front nut so that it pushes the gearbox forward until there is ½ in. to ¾ in. up-and-down movement in the chain run midway between the two sprockets.

Tighten the gearbox top and bottom bolts and operate the kick-starter to check for the tightest point of chain tension. There should be a minimum up-and-down movement of ½ in. to ¾ in. The primary chain must not be excessively tightened. Tighten the drawbolt front nut against the stop so that it tends to push the gearbox forward all the time, and tighten the rear nut just enough to prevent its becoming lost. By doing this backlash in the adjusting mechansim will be taken up so as to hold the gearbox forward against the greater pull of the secondary chain.

Note that the pull of the secondary chain is always greater than that of the primary chain and can move the gearbox back slightly after a jerky start, a very quick gear-change, or if a pillion passenger is carried, if the tension of the secondary chain has been set excessively tight with the weight of the machine only on the wheels. In other words, any final adjusting movement should always be made in a *forward* direction.

**Secondary Chain Adjustment (1955 Models).** It is advisable to check the tension of the secondary chain about every 1,000 miles, and make an adjustment if the chain has stretched. An adjustment is also necessary after re-tensioning the primary chain. Before checking the tension of the secondary chain it is advisable to check the tension of the primary chain (*see* page 91) in case this chain also requires adjustment.

On all 1955 "swinging arm" models with Girling rear-suspension units check the tension of the secondary chain with both wheels resting on the ground and someone seated on the saddle or dualseat. With the chain in its tightest position the total up-and-down movement at the centre of the chain run should be ¾ in. to 1 in. The tightest position for the chain is when the Girling rear-suspension units are compressed to the *mid-stroke position* so that the gearbox mainshaft, pivot fork bolt, and rear wheel spindle are exactly in line.

On all 1955 models to adjust the secondary chain, first slacken slightly both rear-wheel spindle nuts and unscrew the knurled adjuster-nut on the rear-brake rod. Also loosen the two drawbolt adjuster lock-nuts. Then with the appropriate spanner turn both drawbolt adjuster-nuts *clockwise the same amount* until the chain is correctly tensioned. Afterwards securely tighten both rear-wheel spindle nuts and the two lock-nuts on the drawbolts. Finally adjust the rear brake (*see* page 105) and check the alignment of the front and rear wheel (*see* page 112) if in any doubt about this.

**Secondary Chain Adjustment (1956 Onwards).** All 1956 and later models have "swinging arm" rear suspension and the tension of the secondary chain should be checked about every 1,000 miles and a chain adjustment made if excessive slackness exists. An adjustment should also

GENERAL MAINTENANCE 93

always be made after re-tensioning the primary chain. It is advisable to check and if necessary adjust primary chain tension *before* dealing with the secondary chain. With both wheels resting on the ground and with the chain in its tightest position (with Girling or Armstrong rear-suspension units compressed to the *mid-stroke position*), there should be a total up-and-down movement of ¾ in. to 1 in. in the centre of the chain run. Someone must, of course, be sitting on the dualseat or astride the rear

FIG. 42. SECONDARY CHAIN AND REAR BRAKE ADJUSTMENT PROVIDED ON ALL 1956 AND LATER MODELS

1. Rear wheel spindle nut.
2. Hand adjuster on rear-brake rod.
3. Lock-nut for adjuster screw 4.
4. Adjuster screw for tensioning chain.

number plate cuff. Check the whip of the chain with the fingers and make an adjustment if necessary. This should be effected as described below.

Referring to Fig. 42, slacken slightly (about half a turn) the rear-wheel spindle nuts (*1*) to enable the hub spindle to move backwards or forwards in the rear fork ends. Also unscrew the hand adjuster (*2*) on the rear-brake rod, and the two adjuster screw lock-nuts (*3*). Now press down hard on the bottom run of the secondary chain to bring the wheel spindle into firm contact with the two adjuster screws (*4*). Then with someone sitting on the dualseat, or astride the rear number-plate cuff, turn each adjuster screw *anti-clockwise* an equal amount until the chain is correctly tensioned. Afterwards firmly tighten both wheel-spindle nuts and the two adjuster screw lock-nuts. When tightening these lock-nuts it is sometimes necessary to hold the adjuster screws with a second spanner to prevent their turning. Finally adjust the rear brake (*see* page 105) and if in any doubt about wheel alignment, check this (*see* page 112).

**Chain Wear.** Renewal of a primary or secondary chain is recommended as soon as it stretches more than a quarter of an inch per foot. A convenient method of determining chain stretch is to clean the chain in paraffin, lay the chain on a table or bench, close up a foot length of the chain, measure its length, pull the links apart, and again measure the chain for length. The difference between the two lengths is, of course, the distance the chain has stretched.

Another good test for chain wear is to hold the chain sideways and check various lengths for curvature on attempting to bend the chain very

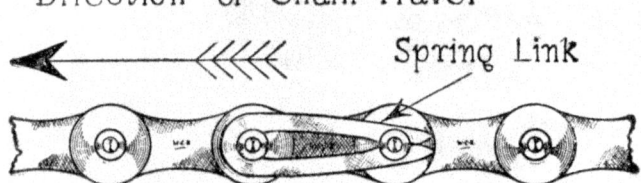

FIG. 43. WHEN CONNECTING A PRIMARY OR SECONDARY CHAIN ALWAYS FIT THE SPRING LINK AS SHOWN ABOVE

gently. With a new chain or one in good condition there should be almost no curvature.

To keep chain wear at its minimum always make sure that it is adequately lubricated (*see* page 25). Also never run with a chain excessively tightened; this greatly accelerates wear. It is preferable to run with a chain slightly on the slack side, provided that this does not cause a primary or secondary chain to make contact with part of the chain case or chain guard. Such contact is usually indicated by an intermittent metallic tap.

**When Fitting a Chain.** When fitting a new secondary chain, fitting is greatly facilitated by joining one end of the new chain to one end of the old chain. The old chain can then be used to pull the new chain into position over the sprockets.

Whenever you join up a primary or secondary chain it is advisable to join its ends on the clutch sprocket or brake drum sprocket respectively; the sprocket teeth will hold the ends in position and facilitate fitting the spring link. Never omit to fit this link with its closed end facing the direction of chain travel as shown in Fig. 43. Should you fit the spring link with its open end facing the direction of chain travel, there is a considerable risk (a dangerous one) of the open end fouling some obstruction and causing the chain to become disconnected. Note that the spring link is not flat, but has a convex and concave side. It should be fitted with the convex side on the outside. The side plate is then held snugly against the bushes of the inner links.

## THE OIL-BATH CHAIN CASE

**To Remove Oil-bath Chain Case (1955-7) Models).** Remove the footrests, the footrest rod, and the rear-brake pedal. Then remove the large nut which secures the outer portion of the oil-bath, and detach the latter. Next remove the clutch-spring screws, the clutch springs, and the cups. There are three of each of these members. Also remove the clutch outerplate, the clutch thrust-rod, and the clutch retaining-nut. When unscrewing this nut, depress the foot gear-change to engage top gear and get someone

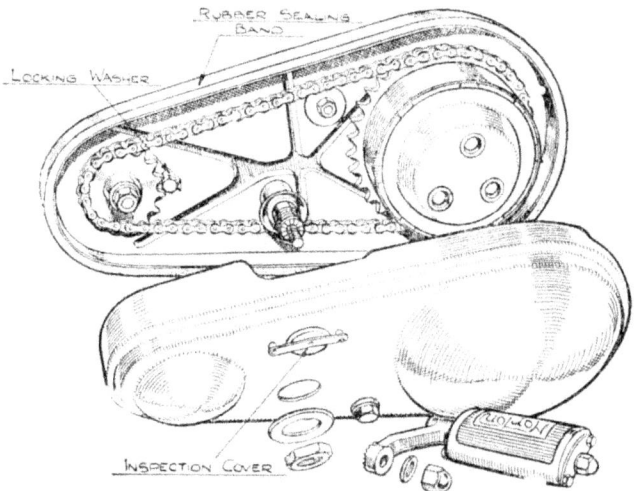

Fig. 44. The 1955-7 Oil-Bath Chain Case with its Outer Portion Removed

to hold the rear wheel. After removing the clutch retaining-nut, withdraw the clutch body; a special tool is obtainable for withdrawing it.

With a claw-type extractor remove the engine sprocket. This sprocket, the clutch, and the primary chain can be removed together. Finally remove the inner portion of the oil-bath which is secured by two bolts and two nuts, bolts being used to secure it to the crankcase and secondary-chain guard, and nuts to secure it to the engine plate and gearbox pivot-bolt.

**To Replace Oil-bath Chain Case (1955-7 Models).** Reassemble the oil-bath in the reverse order to that used for removal. Examine the rubber washer fitted round the flange of the inner portion. This washer comprises an oil seal which must be in good condition to prevent oil leakage. If the band has stretched it is permissible to cut out the necessary amount if the joined ends are placed on the top run of the chain case. When assembly is complete, replenish the oil-bath chain case with suitable oil (*see* page 25) to the level of the plug located near the bottom of the outer portion of the oil-bath.

**To Remove Oil-bath Chain Case (1958–65 Models).** Remove the rear brake pedal by withdrawing the jaw-joint pin and unscrewing the grease nipple from the pedal boss. When doing this be careful not to push the

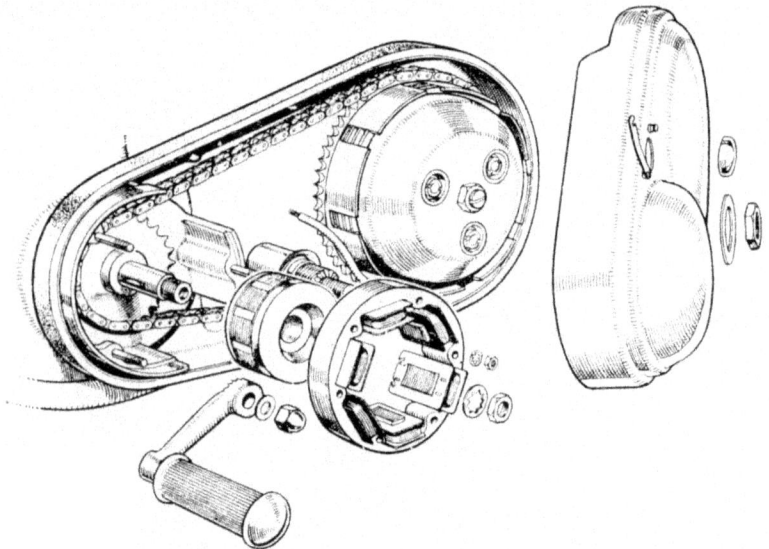

FIG. 45. THE 1958–65 OIL-BATH CHAIN CASE WITH ITS OUTER PORTION REMOVED

The alternator rotor and stator are also shown removed. The removal of these items is, of course, rarely necessary unless the oil-bath has to be removed.

pedal down farther than it normally travels, otherwise the pedal return-spring housed in the pedal boss will be strained and need renewal. Remove the near-side footrest and the large nut screwed on to the footrest tube ($\frac{11}{16}$ in. Whit. hex.). This enables you to withdraw the outer cover exposing the driving chain, the clutch, and the a.c. generator, as shown in Fig. 45. Remove the three nuts holding the stator and withdraw it from its studs, drawing the cable carefully through the grommet in the rear part of the chain case until the stator can be rested safely on the rear engine-plates. Remove the mainshaft nut and the rotor from the mainshaft.

Now remove the primary chain and withdraw the engine sprocket, using a sprocket extractor. Remove the three clutch-spring nuts, springs, and cups, and the clutch pressure-plate. Engage top gear and obtain assistance to hold the rear wheel while the clutch retaining nut is being slackened.

# GENERAL MAINTENANCE

The rear brake can be held on with a ring spanner fitted over the cam-spindle nut.

Having removed the clutch-centre nut, withdraw the clutch assembly; it is on a parallel spline, but if tight a special tool can be obtained from the Norton Service Dept. Remove the three countersunk "Allen" screws which secure the stator housing to the crankcase. The inner part of the chain case is now held by three screws at the front end, by the nut on the gearbox near-side bottom bolt, and by the nut on the hexagon-spacer stud on the near-side engine/gearbox plate. Having removed these nuts and bolts the inner half of the chain case can be withdrawn from the crankcase. A paper washer is fitted between the crankcase and chain case and requires renewal if damaged.

**To Replace Oil-bath Chain Case (1958–65 Models).** Reassemble the oil-bath chain case in the reverse order of dismantling. See that the slots in the stator housing are positioned correctly so as to pass the chain, and fit the chain spring-link so that its *closed* end points in the direction of chain travel and with its convex side outwards. Do not fit the outer portion of the oil-bath chain case until the clutch has been adjusted if necessary (*see* page 98). Observe that the rubber sealing band has a thin lip on one edge only. This must be on the *outer* diameter of the band and towards the oil-bath chain case cover. If the band has stretched it is permissible to cut a piece out and join the band with wire, provided the joint is positioned on the top side of the chain case.

Fit the stator with the edge from which the leads are taken *innermost*, drawing surplus cable through to behind the inner portion. Replace the outer cover of the oil-bath chain case, giving the rim a few blows with the ball of the hand or a rubber mallet while tightening the nut. Avoid excessive tightening of this nut, otherwise some distortion of the chain case may occur. With the nut properly tightened, only one or two threads should protrude through the nut. Replenish the case (*see* page 25).

## THE CLUTCH

**Clutch Adjustment.** On all models always keep the clutch adjusted so that there is about $\frac{1}{8}$ in. free movement of the clutch control-cable at the handlebar end. This clearance gradually decreases as the friction material used in the clutch plates wears. Absence of backlash in the control cable causes the clutch to slip and accelerates wear and tear of its plates. Excessive backlash in the control cable usually results in some clutch drag and general inefficiency of clutch operation. Proper adjustment of the clutch is essential to obtain quick and perfect gear changing.

**To Adjust Burman Clutch (1955–6 Models).** A Burman gearbox and clutch is fitted to all 1955 and some 1956 Norton Twins. Should a clutch cable adjustment be necessary, loosen the lock-nut on the off-side of the gearbox and then turn the cable adjuster as required to give the necessary backlash at the handlebar lever. Should it be found impossible to effect an adequate adjustment by this means, or should the cable adjustment result in the clutch worm-lever assuming an unsuitable position, make a further adjustment by means of the worm lever. This is accessible on removing the two screws which secure the oval cover to the gearbox outer cover. The oval cover forms an outrigger bearing for the clutch worm and is usually rather a tight fit in the outer cover.

To remove a tight oval cover, tap round it gently until the ends stand away from the gearbox outer-cover and provide two lips into which suitable levers can be inserted. When levering-off the oval cover avoid using excessive force, otherwise it may become distorted.

To make a worm-lever adjustment, slacken the cable adjuster right down and turn the lever on the shank of the worm after releasing the pinch bolt and while holding the shank by means of the slot machined across its end. Turn the clutch worm-lever *anti-clockwise* until it is about 45 degrees below the horizontal. Then effect the necessary cable adjustment and verify that the angle between the cable and worm lever is approximately a right-angle with the clutch fully disengaged. No adjustment for clutch-spring pressure is provided, and the clutch-spring pins should always be kept screwed *fully home*.

**To Adjust A.M.C. Clutch (1956–65 Models).** An A.M.C. gearbox and clutch is fitted to some 1956 and all 1957 and later Twins. The clutch provided has friction material bonded on to the driven plates except on earlier gearboxes where the driving plates and the clutch sprocket have friction inserts.

With the clutch control cable slackened off, there should be $\frac{1}{8}$ in. free movement in the small operating lever in the kick-starter case. This lever is shown on the extreme right of Fig. 46. If there is more or less than $\frac{1}{8}$ in. free movement, remove the outer half of the oil-bath chain case (*see* pages 95–6). Loosen the lock-nut ($\frac{7}{16}$ in. Whitworth hexagon) on the adjuster screw located in the centre of the aluminium pressure-plate and set the screw as required. If it is first screwed in until it is hard on the push-rod and then slackened back half a turn, this should give about the right amount of free movement in the small operating lever.

Tighten the lock-nut for the adjuster screw and adjust the external cable adjuster (shown at (7) in Fig. 39) on top of the gearbox outer cover so that there is about $\frac{1}{8}$ in. free movement of the cable at the handlebar end. The clutch pressure-plate should now come off squarely and rotate true laterally when the kick-starter is operated with the clutch withdrawn. If it does not do so, adjust the clutch spring adjuster-nuts individually as required.

Should you for any reason dismantle the clutch, check that the nut which secures the clutch centre to the gearbox mainshaft is tight before replacing the pressure plate, springs, etc. If you fit a new clutch lever to the handlebars, make sure that it has the correct centres for the cable nipple and the fulcrum pin. These should be ⅞ in.

**Dismantling Burman Clutch (1955–6 Models).** First remove the outer portion of the oil-bath chain case (*see* page 95). Also remove the clutch body with the special tool available. If it is desired to inspect the driving slots in the clutch sprocket, remove the steel band which is pressed round

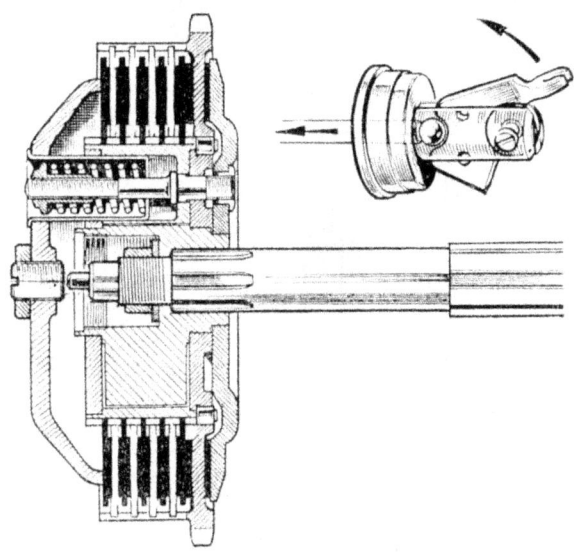

Fig. 46. Sectioned View of Clutch on 1960 and Later A.M.C. Gearboxes

Inserts were fitted to the driving plates of all clutches fitted to 1956–9 A.M.C. gearboxes. In other respects all 1956–65 A.M.C. clutches are identical. On the right is shown the small push-rod operating lever housed in the kick-starter case.

the clutch sprocket. If you intend to dismantle the clutch plates only, the steel band can be left in position. This steel band, by the way, has proved to be of no value and can safely be scrapped.

To remove the clutch plates detach the circlip which holds the plates on to the clutch body and withdraw the plates. There are six plain-steel plates and five steel plates with Ferodo inserts. Now remove the clutch sprocket. NOTE: the circlip causes plates to stick; scrap it.

Referring to Fig. 47, grip an old gearbox mainshaft (if available) between the jaws of a vice, with its splined end above the jaws, and fit the clutch body to the gearbox mainshaft. Remove all three screws holding the front cover-plate and tap the plate round until a screwdriver can be used to prise it off (*see* Fig. 48). Now remove the clutch cover-plate and the shock-absorber rubbers (*see* Fig. 47). Remove the rubbers with a large "C" spanner. Place the spanner over the body so as to engage the splines as illustrated in Fig. 47. Compress the large rubbers while removing the smaller ones. The length of the spanner should be such that the load can be taken by your thighs while both hands are free to remove the shock-absorber rubbers. A good substitute for a "C" spanner is an old plain-steel clutch plate with a handle attached. To remove the large and smaller rubbers it is advisable to use a sharp-pointed tool.

Remove the clutch body from the mainshaft and replace it in the reverse

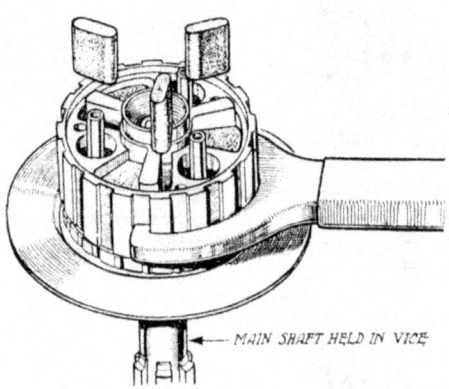

FIG. 47. REMOVAL OF SHOCK-ABSORBER RUBBERS FROM A.M.C. CLUTCH BODY WITH A "C" SPANNER

position. Then remove the nuts from the three studs on the back cover-plate. Finally separate the back plate, roller race, back cover, and clutch body.

**Inspecting Burman Clutch Parts (1955–7 Models).** When occasion is had to strip down the clutch (*see* Fig. 49) during a complete overhaul make a close inspection of the various components. Visually inspect the inserts in each friction plate. They must be proud of the steel plate in which they are fitted. If you fit new inserts see that they are all level and flat, and that they all contact the adjacent plain-steel plates. The fitting of only a few new friction inserts is very unsatisfactory. It is advisable, if possible, to replace friction-insert plates with either new clutch plates or plates which have been reconditioned.

Look for wear on the drive of the plates. The drive of the plain-steel plates is taken on their inside circumference, but that for the friction-insert plates is taken on their outside circumference.

The splines on the clutch centre and the corresponding splines on the plain-steel plates seldom show signs of wear, but this does not always apply to the tongues on the friction-insert plates. These tongues sometimes wear and occasionally they bite into the driven part of the clutch sprocket. The only ill effect is the creation of a little backlash in the clutch control. This is of no consequence.

Inspect the plain-steel plates for signs of roughness, especially in the case of the back plate. Verify the condition of the bearing rollers, race, and

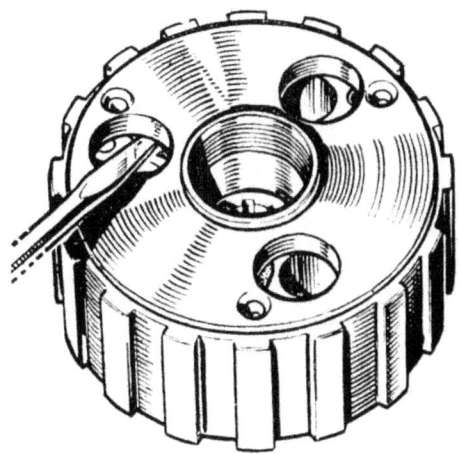

FIG. 48. EXPOSING THE CLUTCH SHOCK-ABSORBER RUBBERS FROM BODY OF A.M.C. CLUTCH (1956-65)

The three cover-plate securing screws have been removed.

cage. See if the back cover-plate is worn by the clutch centre. Also inspect the shock-absorber rubbers for evidence of cracking or softening.

**Assembling Burman Clutch (1955-6 Models).** Assemble the clutch back cover-plate to the body. Check that the mating holes are in alignment and that the spring studs are an easy fit. Replace the clutch-body front cover and fit the large shock-absorber rubbers. Compress these and fit the smaller ones. Replace the clutch-body centre and tighten the screws. Fit the roller race on the back cover-plate, fit the clutch back-plate, and replace the back-plate spring studs. Fit nuts to the studs and tighten them, finally locking the nuts with a centre-punch. Test the roller race for freedom on its track and apply a little anti-centrifuge grease.

Replace the steel band on the clutch sprocket, making sure that the latter does not become distorted. Check all clutch plates for free movement and fit the clutch sprocket to the body. Rotate the sprocket on the race to verify that it runs freely. Next assemble the clutch plates on the sprocket and body. The correct order of fitting is: plain-steel plate; insert plate; plain steel plate, etc. The bevelled edges of the plates must be *towards* the sprocket. Turn the sprocket to check that the plates are quite free.

Fit the plate retaining-circlip where provided and assemble the clutch to the gearbox mainshaft. Replace the clutch thrust-rod, the clutch outer plate, spring cups, springs, and spring pins. Tighten the latter *fully*, and then complete the assembly by replacing the outer portion of the oil-bath chain case (*see* page 95).

**Dismantling A.M.C. Clutch (1956 Onwards).** First remove the outer portion of the oil-bath chain case (*see* page 97). Remove the clutch spring

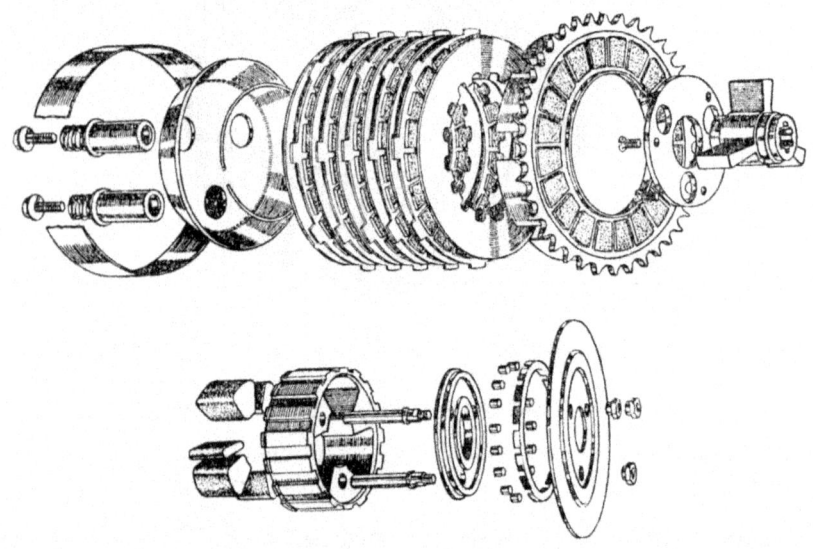

FIG. 49. EXPLODED VIEW OF BURMAN MULTI-PLATE CLUTCH FITTED TO 1955 AND SOME 1956 MODELS

The upper components should be regarded as being in line with and to the left of the bottom assembly.

adjuster-nuts with a divided screwdriver, or else use a small screwdriver on one side only. Each screw has a locking "pip" under its head and considerable torque may be necessary to get over it during the first one or two revolutions. The clutch pressure-plate can now be withdrawn. Remove the clutch plates and note that the first plate (1960 onwards) has bonded friction material on one side only and must therefore always be the end plate. Disconnect the primary chain and remove the clutch chain wheel. Engage top gear and unscrew the clutch centre (right-hand thread), using a $\frac{7}{16}$ in. Whitworth hexagon box-spanner. Remove both the nut and the spring washer. Now withdraw the clutch centre from the gearbox splined-mainshaft.

To dismantle the clutch shock-absorber rubbers proceed as described on page 100 for the 1955–6 Burman clutch, noting Figs. 47 and 48. Then remove the body from the mainshaft, take out the "spider" or shock-absorber centre and turn the body upside down on the bench. Remove the three nuts on the spring studs and separate the back plate, the roller race, and the clutch body.

**Examining A.M.C. Clutch Parts (1956 Onwards).** Inspect the driven plates with their inserts or bonded strips (1960 onwards) of friction material and make sure that none are missing. Clean them thoroughly with a stiff brush and petrol. Place the driving plates together and check that they are flat. These should be of the "pin-point planished" type, i.e. they should have small "pop" marks all over them. Plates so treated will not buckle at high temperatures. The splines on the clutch body and the bonded plates which drive the body rarely show any signs of wear, but the tongues on the plain driving plates may become worn and may have cut slots in the chain wheel. When the clutch is operated this wear can obstruct free movement of the clutch plates. The remedy is to file or grind the tongues on the plates square, also the driving edge of the slots in the chain wheel. No ill effect of this occurs other than a slight degree of backlash when the clutch is engaged or disengaged.

Inspect the roller race, the rollers, and the cage. Examine the race plate, face, and bore for wear by the clutch-body centre or "spider". Examine the clutch shock-absorber rubbers for signs of softening or cracking. Also look at the "spider" itself for signs of wear on the race plate and cover-plate diameters. Inspect the internal splines for any fractures.

**Assembling A.M.C. Clutch (1956 Onwards).** Fit the race plate to the clutch body, making sure that the holes in the plate are in line with the holes in the body, and that the spring studs are an easy fit. Fit the roller cage, the rollers, and the back plate. Replace the shock-absorber centre or "spider" in the clutch body and lock the nuts on the studs. Fit the large rubbers, followed by the smaller ones. Fit the cover plate and three screws (with countersunk or cheese heads). Now test the roller race for freeness on its track and apply a little medium or anti-centrifuge grease.

Check all the clutch plates on the body and in the sprocket (clutch case) for freeness. Next fit the clutch sprocket to the body, revolve the sprocket on the race to check free movement, and fit all the plates in the following sequence. First fit an inserted or a double-sided bonded driven plate, followed by a plain driving plate and so on in alternate order until the last inserted or bonded plate (single-sided) is fitted. This should present its plain-steel side to the pressure plate.

Fit the clutch to the gearbox mainshaft, fit the spring washer and nut, engage top gear, and tighten the nut. Finally fit the clutch push-rod, the clutch pressure-plate, the spring cups, the springs, and the spring adjuster-nuts. Screw up the nuts until the studs are all flush with the ends of the nuts, and adjust as necessary to ensure square withdrawal of the clutch pressure-plate. Replace the outer portion of the oil-bath chain case as described on page 97.

## THE GEARBOX

**Lubrication and Overhaul.** As in the case of the primary and secondary chains, the teeth of the four-speed gearbox are subjected to huge stresses. Gearbox lubrication, dealt with on page 24, should therefore never be neglected. The gearbox should satisfactorily perform its duties for thousands of miles provided that you take reasonable care when gear changing, top-up the Burman (1955-6) or A.M.C. (1956-65) gearbox with summer grade engine oil every 1,000 miles, and change the oil every 5,000 miles.

If subsequent to a very big mileage, or because of some neglect, the gearbox operates noisily and gear changing becomes difficult it is advisable to remove the gearbox (*see* later paragraph) and have it thoroughly overhauled by Matchless Motor Cycles Ltd., Service Dept. (Norton), or by a reputable firm handling Norton spares and repairs. Gearbox overhaul is a job seldom undertaken by the average motor-cyclist and for this reason and because of the limited space at the author's disposal, gearbox dismantling, inspection, and assembly instructions are not included in this handbook. Some useful instructions are, however, given in the official Norton instruction book supplied with each new machine.

**Removing Gearbox from "Featherbed" Frame (1955-65 Models).** On all 1955 and later "Dominators" having a "featherbed" type frame it is not practicable to remove the gearbox separately from the frame. Remove the engine and gearbox *as a single unit* (*see* page 90). You can then readily detach the gearbox from the engine.

## FRONT AND REAR BRAKES

Note the advice given on pages 4 and 29 with regard to the proper use and lubrication of the front and rear brakes. This section deals with their adjustment, dismantling, and assembling. As regards adjustment necessary to compensate for wear of the brake-shoe linings, always keep both brakes adjusted to give maximum leverage and efficiency. *The brake-shoe linings should be just clear of the brake drums but close enough to ensure immediate contact on brake application.*

**Front Brake Adjustment.** On all Norton Twins the front brake cable has finger adjustment. Referring to Fig. 50, if an adjustment is necessary because of lining wear, slacken the knurled lock-nut (*1*) fitted to the cable stop on the front brake cover-plate and screw the knurled adjuster (*2*) *outwards* until brake adjustment is correct as previously referred to. Afterwards firmly tighten the knurled lock-nut.

After numerous brake adjustments have been made the altered position of the brake-shoe expander lever results in some loss of leverage. An

FIG. 50. FRONT BRAKE ADJUSTMENT (ALL MODELS)
1. Knurled lock-nut for 2.     2. Knurled finger adjuster.
3. Brake-shoe expander lever.

effective remedy is to disconnect the cable "U" clip and reverse the brake-shoe expander lever (*3*). To improve the efficiency of the front brake, unscrew the nut on the expander-lever spindle a few turns, squeeze the handlebar lever firmly, and simultaneously retighten the spindle nut. This will centralize the brake shoes. Always keep both brakes properly adjusted. Good braking power is needed to cope with emergencies. Test the brakes occasionally at about 30 m.p.h.

**Rear Brake Adjustment.** All Norton models have a knurled hand-adjuster on the rear-brake operating rod as shown at (*2*) in Fig. 42. Besides making a routine adjustment necessitated because of wear of the brake-shoe linings, rear brake adjustment is always necessary after re-tensioning the secondary chain.

If the rear-brake pedal is depressed beyond its normal movement the return spring (usually located in the pedal boss) will stretch and become inefficient. On 1955-65 (and some earlier models) you can adjust the position of the pedal to some extent by releasing the pedal spindle and adjusting the pedal stop provided. If you have previously completely dismantled the rear brake, centralize the brake shoes by slackening the nut on the rear wheel spindle (near side) and then tightening it while applying strong foot pressure to the rear-brake pedal.

**To Dismantle Brakes.** For dismantling all 1955-65 and some earlier front and rear brakes first remove the brake plate from the brake drum. Also remove the nut and washer from the brake-shoe expander-lever spindle and withdraw the expander lever. Next extract the springs which contract the brake shoes. While placing a screwdriver against one of the spring hooks and holding the screwdriver in place with one hand, knock the top of the screwdriver with the palm of the other hand until the spring is pushed off the lug on the brake shoe. It may fly off, so be careful not to lose it.

Now turn back the tab-washer and unscrew the two hexagon-headed set-screws securing the brake shoes to their pivot pins. Withdraw the pivot pin tie-plate and remove both brake shoes. Note that the washer on the rear-brake expander, together with the rim on the brake cover-plate, prevents removal of the rear brake shoes from their pivot pins *unless the brake linings are badly worn.* Removal of the expander cam enables the shoes to be withdrawn from the cover plate. Then remove the cam and expander (cam) lever spindle. If the expander-lever spindle nut has been overtightened, the end of the spindle may have swelled, causing it to be tight in its bush. The remedy is to ease down with some emery cloth the spindle end immediately behind the flats. If the cam spindle will pass through the bush in spite of stiffness, it is simpler to ease down the end of the spindle *after* removing it.

**To Assemble Brakes.** To assemble the front and rear brakes (all 1955-65 models), proceed as follows. First remove all traces of dirt and rust from the expander cam and the shoe pivot-pins. Apply a slight smear of grease and continue with the assembly. This is much facilitated by holding the brake cover-plate in a smooth-jaw vice, clamping it by the torque stops. First fit the brake shoes, the tie-plate, the tab-washer, and the set-screws. Renew the tab-washer if it has been used on more than one occasion.

Now assemble the brake-shoe springs. Anchor the end of each spring farthest away from you, use a length of strong string in the free end of the spring, stretch the spring with one hand, and guide the spring on to its anchorage with the other hand. Alternatively use a narrow-blade screwdriver. Finally fit the brake-shoe expander lever spindle, the expander lever, and its securing nut and washer.

**Brake Linings.** If either brake tends to squeak or is harsh in action, remove the brake-shoe assembly and file each lining thin for about 1 in. from each end. This slightly reduces the effective area of brake lining but results in much smoother braking without any appreciable loss in efficiency. Rough up hard, smooth linings with a file and clean oily ones with some petrol.

### WHEELS AND TYRES

**Hub Lubrication.** Observe the instructions given on page 29 for greasing the front and rear hubs. Every 10,000 miles remove both wheels, dismantle the hubs, and clean and repack their bearings with suitable grease.

**Wheel Bearings Have No Adjustment.** Journal-type ball bearings are provided for both wheels of all 1949-65 Norton Twins. No adjustment is provided or necessary.

**Removing Front Wheel (1955 Models Onwards).** Referring to Fig. 50, place your Norton on both its stands or, where provided, on its centre stand, and disconnect the front brake cable from the expander lever (*3*). Also disconnect the knurled finger-adjuster (*2*) from the brake cover-plate after slackening the knurled lock-nut (*1*). Now remove the wheel-spindle nut on the off-side and also loosen the pinch-bolt in the near-side fork-slider end. Then support the front wheel with the left hand and pull out the wheel spindle by means of a tommy-bar inserted through the hole in the head of the spindle. When the wheel is removed be careful not to allow the brake cover-plate to fall from the brake drum. If this happens its bevelled edge may be damaged.

**To Replace Front Wheel (1955 Models Onwards).** Replace the wheel in the reverse order of removal. As the front wheel is positioned in the telescopic forks see that the torque stop on the brake cover-plate engages the slot in the off-side fork leg. With the right hand insert the wheel spindle from the near-side after first removing all rust and greasing it. Having tightened the wheel-spindle securing nut on the off-side, lock the pinch bolt on the near-side fork-slider end. Avoid over-tightening the fork-slider pinch bolt, otherwise a fracture may result. Reconnect the front-brake cable to the expander lever and adjust the front brake correctly (*see* page 105).

Should the action of the telescopic front-forks be found rather stiff after replacing the front wheel, loosen the pinch nut on the near-side and work the forks up and down so as to align their tubes. Afterwards carefully retighten the pinch nut.

**Removing Rear Wheel (1954 Models).** Many 1954 models have "swinging arm" rear suspension and quickly-detachable rear wheels (with small diameter hubs not of the light-alloy type).

Prior to removing the rear wheel it is sufficient on models with "swinging arm" rear suspension to raise the hinged end of the mudguard. To remove the tail-piece it is necessary after disconnecting the stop-tail lamp leads to remove the two bolts securing it to the main portion of the mudguard, and also the two bolts holding the stays at the bottom of the tail-piece. To raise the hinged end of a rear mudguard it is only necessary to disconnect the wiring and then remove the end bolt from each side lifting-handle.

To remove *a rear wheel of the quickly-detachable type* (without a full width light-alloy hub) from a 1954 machine *with "swinging arm" rear suspension* is straightforward. Having placed the Norton on its rear or centre stand and dealt with the rear mudguard as previously mentioned, disconnect the speedometer driving-cable. Next remove the rear-wheel spindle, distance piece, and speedometer-drive gearbox. Then remove the nuts from the three hub studs and draw the wheel off these studs. The rear wheel can then be entirely removed, leaving the brake drum in position.

The procedure for removing a *quickly-detachable rear wheel*, with hub which is *not of the full width light-alloy type complete with brake drum*, necessitates the removal of the mudguard tail-piece, the secondary chain, the adjuster nut on the rear-brake rod, and the anchorage bolt securing the brake anchorage arm to the frame. Then slacken both spindle nuts and remove the rear wheel and brake drum assembly from the frame.

**To Replace Rear Wheel (1954 Models).** Reverse the removal procedure. When fitting *a quickly-detachable rear wheel*, be sure to tighten the three nuts on the hub studs evenly and firmly. When replacing *a rear wheel not of the quickly-detachable type*, see that the fork ends are lying reasonably parallel to each other. When positioning the wheel make certain that the ears of each adjuster stirrup lie flat against the sides of the rear-fork end. Also see that the cupped adjuster-washer is located on the small shoulder at the open end of the fork-end slot. In addition check that the anchor pad on the rear brake cover-plate enters the slot on the inside of the near-side fork end.

On all models when replacing *a complete rear wheel assembly* (with brake drum attached) make sure that the wheel spindle bears hard up against the chain adjusters, that the chain spring-link is fitted correctly (*see* Fig. 43), that both wheels are in true alignment (*see* page 112), and that the speedometer drive is connected properly.

**Removing Rear Wheel (1955 Models Onwards).** All 1955 and later Nortons have "*swinging arm*" *rear suspension* and quickly-detachable rear wheels with (all Norton "Dominators") light-alloy hubs of large diameter. Remove *a quickly-detachable rear wheel with full width light-alloy hub* as described below.

Place your Norton Twin on its centre stand. If it is a de Luxe model remove the rear number-plate. Remove the three rubber plugs from the off-side of the rear hub and with a box or socket spanner unscrew and remove the three exposed sleeve-nuts which secure the rear wheel to the brake drum. Next unscrew the off-side portion of the wheel spindle and withdraw it. Now remove the spacer and the speedometer-drive gearbox, allowing the latter to hang on its cable. Then withdraw the rear wheel from the brake drum by pulling it towards the off-side. It should readily come away clear of the three studs projecting from the brake drum, leaving the latter and the secondary chain undisturbed.

Note that on very many "Dominators" of standard type, especially more recent models, which do not have a hinged or a detachable mudguard tail-piece (see page 108), it is necessary to withdraw the rear wheel with the right hand from the off-side while standing on the near-side and inclining the motor-cycle slightly towards you on its centre stand.

On de Luxe models if the tyre is punctured and therefore flat, withdraw the rear wheel through the space left by removing the rear number-plate. On the same-type models if the rear tyre is inflated it may be necessary, as with standard type models, to incline the motorcycle slightly towards you in order to remove the rear wheel.

To remove *a quickly-detachable rear wheel complete with brake drum*, remove the secondary-chain case or guard and disconnect the chain. Also remove the knurled adjuster-nut from the brake rod, but do not push the brake pedal down to withdraw the rod from the roller. Disconnect the "dead" lead from the stop-lamp switch and the brake torque arm from the frame (1955-6 models) or rear fork-end slot (1957 on). Also disconnect the speedometer-drive cable and loosen both ends of the two-piece wheel spindle. The wheel can then be withdrawn from the rear fork ends. Remove it as previously described but note that it may be necessary to remove the off-side silencer because of the greater width caused by the off-side portion of the wheel spindle remaining in the hub.

**To Replace Rear Wheel (1955 Models Onwards).** Reverse the removal procedure and, if fitting *a quickly-detachable rear wheel complete with brake drum*, see that the torque stop (1957 on) on the brake cover-plate engages properly with the slot in the near-side fork end. Engage the brake rod in the expander-lever roller and push the wheel spindle hard up against the chain-tension adjuster screws. Position the speedometer gearbox for correct cable take-off angle and tighten both sides of the wheel spindle. Connect the speedometer-drive cable but do not over-tighten the gland nut. Replace the secondary chain, fit its spring link correctly (see Fig. 43), and check its tension (see page 92). Replace the chain case or chain guard and carefully adjust the rear brake (see page 105). If an alteration in chain tension has been found necessary, check wheel alignment (see page 112). Reconnect the stop-lamp switch "dead" lead. On a de Luxe model replace the rear number-plate.

When replacing *a quickly-detachable rear wheel only*, with the brake drum positioned on the machine, incline the motor-cycle as necessary to manœuvre the rear wheel under the mudguard or tail fairing unless a detachable tail-piece is provided. Turn the brake drum by hand so that one of its three studs is approximately in line with the pivoted fork (the "swinging arm"). This will facilitate getting the bearing boss on the hub past the other two studs and fitting the hub to the brake drum.

Fit and tighten the three sleeve-nuts to secure the rear wheel and replace the three rubber plugs. Replace the speedometer-drive gearbox and make sure that its driving dogs engage properly the slots in the hub bearing lock-ring. Position the spacer and fit the off-side part of the divided spindle. Make sure that the washer on this passes the end of the chain-tension adjuster screw in the fork end, and that as the spindle is screwed home its head does not catch on the adjuster screw and bend it. Tighten the spindle and on a de Luxe model replace the rear number-plate. If a detachable tail-piece is provided, replace this.

**Dismantling Wheel Hubs.** On 1955–65 models it is necessary to dismantle the front and rear hubs every 10,000 miles in order to clean and repack their bearings with grease. Dismantling is also necessary after a big mileage so that the brake shoes can be relined or a set of exchange-shoes fitted. Only one type of rear-wheel hub has been fitted from 1955 on, and the appropriate instructions on dismantling and assembling the hub given in the manufacturer's appropriate maintenance manual should be closely followed. Limited space at the author's disposal does not permit of detailed instructions being included in this handbook. Advice on the removal of brake shoes from 1955–65 models is, however, given on page 106.

**Keep Your Tyre Pressures Correct.** Running with incorrectly inflated tyres can increase tyre wear considerably, cause some discomfort, and possibly be a source of danger, especially if the tyre pressures are much below those recommended by Norton Motors Ltd. The rear tyre is liable to suffer irreparable damage if under-inflated for a considerable mileage.

It is advisable to check the pressure of both tyres *weekly* and to pump up the tyres immediately if found to be under inflated. The tyre pressures recommended are given in a later paragraph. For checking tyre pressures some excellent proprietary gauges of the pocket type with pistons calibrated in lb per sq in. are available. Among these are the Dunlop No. 6, the Schrader No. 7750, the Holdtite, and the Romac. After removing each tyre-valve dust cap and depressing the valve pin with the gauge to ascertain tyre pressure, always fit and screw home the dust cap firmly. Dirt or grit entering the valve stem is likely to interfere with the valve action of the small internal spring-controlled plunger (*see* Fig. 51) and cause leakage of air. It is advisable to renew the valve "inside" annually. Use the slotted end of the dust cap as a screwdriver for removing it and fitting a new one.

# GENERAL MAINTENANCE

**Recommended Tyre Pressures (Solo).** The solo tyre pressures recommended by the makers of Nortons are as follows in lb per sq in.

1955–63 497 CC MODEL 88: front, 25; rear, 22.
1956–61 597 CC MODEL 99: front, 25; rear 22.
1962–3 MODEL 650*: front 25; rear, 22.
ALL SPORTS SPECIAL (SS) MODELS*: front, 25; rear, 20.
1964–5 745 CC "ATLAS": front, 24; rear, 20.

Note that where heavy luggage or a pillion passenger is carried it is

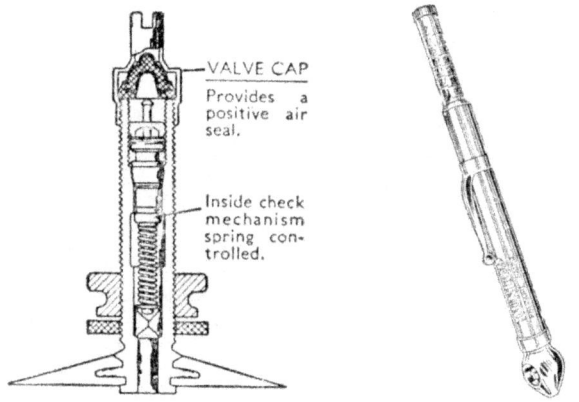

FIG. 51. SHOWING (LEFT) DUNLOP TYRE VALVE AND (RIGHT) DUNLOP NO. 6 POCKET-TYPE PRESSURE GAUGE

advisable to increase the pressure of the rear tyre by several lb per sq in. above the pressure recommended above.

**Some Tyre Hints.** Do not allow your Norton to stand for long periods off its rear or centre stand. This is bad for both wheels and tyres. Never permit your mount to stand on its wheels in a welter of paraffin or oil. This causes tyres to soften and deteriorate quickly.

Occasionally, with the motor-cycle jacked up, inspect both tyres and with a small penknife remove all flints and small stones which are embedded in the rubber treads. If not removed, these may penetrate deeper and ultimately cause a hold-up on the road, possibly in most annoying circumstances.

Note that every 650 cc and SS model is originally fitted with an Avon G.P. rear tyre and a special inner tube. When rear tyre renewal becomes necessary it is most important to fit a new rear tyre of the same type.

* If a 650 cc or a Sports Special Model 88SS or 650SS is ridden on a track or Motorway for long distances at a sustained speed of 110 m.p.h. or more, the pressure of the Avon G.P. tyre should be increased to 30 lb per sq in.

**Wheel Alignment on a Solo Model.** Moving the rear wheel backwards when re-tensioning the secondary chain sometimes upsets wheel alignment. If the rear wheel is not truly aligned with the front one, tyre wear becomes uneven and the motor-cycle becomes less stable on the road. Its steering may be appreciably affected.

To check wheel alignment use a taut piece of string attached to an anchor post or else a straight-edged board (about 6 ft. long, 1 in. wide, and $\frac{1}{2}$ in. thick). Place your Norton on its rear or centre stand so that is is

Fig. 52. Checking Wheel Alignment on a Solo Model

At A is shown a taut piece of string. If the front and rear tyres are of the same section it should contact the two tyres at the four points indicated by white dots. A straight-edged board (*see* text) can alternatively be used for checking wheel alignment which is recommended after re-tensioning the secondary chain. The machine illustrated, by the way, is a 500 cc Model 88SS. The Sports Special Model 650SS is similar except for a hotted-up engine of bigger capacity. A powerful 750 cc "Atlas" completes the 1965-6 "Dominator" range. Optional extras for Norton Sports Specials are a rev. counter, a steering damper, a chain case giving complete enclosure of the secondary chain, and Dolphin fairings.

quite upright and the handlebars are in their normal position. Then position the taut piece of string or board alongside both tyres as shown in Fig. 52. If wheel alignment is correct it should contact each tyre at the front and rear, assuming of course, that both tyres are of the same section. If the rear tyre is of larger section than the front one, due allowance must be made for this; the gaps between the string or board and the front and rear of the front tyre should in this case be exactly equal.

If the front and rear wheels are found not to be in true alignment rectify matters by means of the two chain-adjuster nuts or screws provided at the rear fork ends (*see* page 92).

**Fitting a Sidecar to a "Featherbed" Frame (1955 Onwards).** It is necessary to *reduce the trail* to ensure good handling after fitting a sidecar. A special fork crown and column, and head clip, are available. Because these have different dimensions, new top fork covers with lamp brackets are required. These parts reduce the trail and, with a sidecar outfit properly aligned and set up, produce excellent steering.

The special fork crown and column require a steering damper with two friction discs which centre on a large-diameter boss on the underside of the crown. These parts do not affect the solo crown. There is also a steering damper for the solo crown which has a single friction-disc of

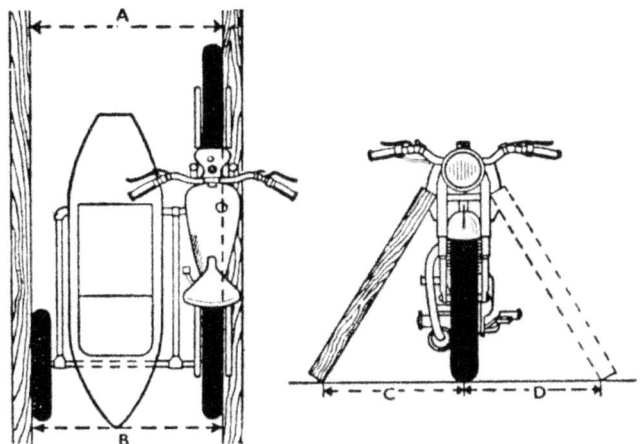

FIG. 53. CHECKING "TOE-IN" ON A SIDECAR OUTFIT AND THE OUTWARD "LEAN" OF THE MOTOR-CYCLE

On most sidecar outfits dimension A should be ¾ in. less than dimension B, and dimension C should be ¾ in. more than dimension D.

different dimensions, and when ordering parts it is important to state for which crown a damper is required.

Stronger front fork springs and rear shock-absorber springs are also available, and should be fitted. Because of the added electrical consumption of sidecar lamps, an a.c. generator may not maintain the battery well charged unless an increased output is obtained as described on page 51.

**Wheel Alignment on a Sidecar Outfit.** To avoid excessive tyre wear and a tendency for skidding it is essential to keep all three wheels properly aligned. The front and rear wheels of the motor-cycle must be kept in true alignment as in the case of a solo machine. An adjustment should be made if necessary by means of the two chain-adjuster nuts or screws provided at the rear fork ends. When checking sidecar wheel alignment it is, however, necessary to use two straight-edged boards instead of one.

The sidecar wheel should "toe-in" to the extent of about ¾ in. and the Norton itself should *lean outwards about ¾ in.* away from the sidecar (*see* Fig. 53). The exact amount of "toe-in" and "lean" required varies slightly according to the design of sidecar fitted, and when attaching a sidecar you should follow precisely the sidecar maker's instructions in regard to this matter and fitting procedure.

## STEERING HEAD ADJUSTMENT

**Why This Adjustment is Important.** On a brand new Norton check the steering head adjustment after covering about 100 miles and subsequently about every 1,000 miles. Two ball bearings are provided and the balls settle down in their races causing some inevitable slackness. If some bearing play develops it is important to eliminate all such play immediately, otherwise the two ball bearings are likely to become damaged through the continuous hammering action of the balls on their races.

When taking up bearing slackness it is essential to avoid over-tightening the bearings. Tight bearings cause the motor-cycle to develop a most unpleasant tendency to roll and to skid readily on slippery road surfaces.

**Checking Steering Head Adjustment.** Slackness in the steering head bearings can usually be diagnosed when the front brake is applied. Test for slackness in the following manner. If your motor-cycle has no centre stand, insert beneath the engine cradle a box or wooden block of sufficient height to raise the front wheel clear of the ground. If it has a centre stand, but this does not raise the front wheel quite clear of the ground, pack up the stand with a suitable piece of wood.

Place the thumb or fingers on the joint between the frame steering-head and the fork-head clip or the rear of the handlebar lug. Then with the other hand try to raise and lower the front wheel and fork assembly. This can conveniently be done with the hand grasping the end of the front mudguard. By this method you can easily tell by feel whether there is slackness in the steering-head bearings.

When the steering head is correctly adjusted there should be no play in the bearings but it should be possible to move the handlebars from full left lock over to full right lock without any friction.

**To Adjust Steering Head (All Models).** After checking that play exists in the steering head bearings it is a simple matter, with the front wheel raised clear of the ground, to make the necessary adjustment. This is shown clearly in Fig. 54.

First with a box or ring type spanner slacken slightly the lock-nut (6) on top of the steering column (9) after removing the steering damper if fitted. Most 1959–63 models have a $\frac{11}{16}$ in. Whitworth hexagonal domed lock-nut, and on some machines removal of this domed lock-nut is made more easy by first removing the handlebars from their mounting clips. Also loosen the two pinch-stud nuts (*10*) which clamp the fork-leg main tubes to the fork crown. Then eliminate all bearing slackness by turning *clockwise* as required (using an open-ended spanner) the bearing adjuster nut (8) located on the steering column below the fork-head clip or the handlebar lug.

A $\frac{13}{16}$ in. Whitworth hexagonal bearing adjuster-nut is provided on 1959–65 models and a suitable open-ended Norton spanner to use (not

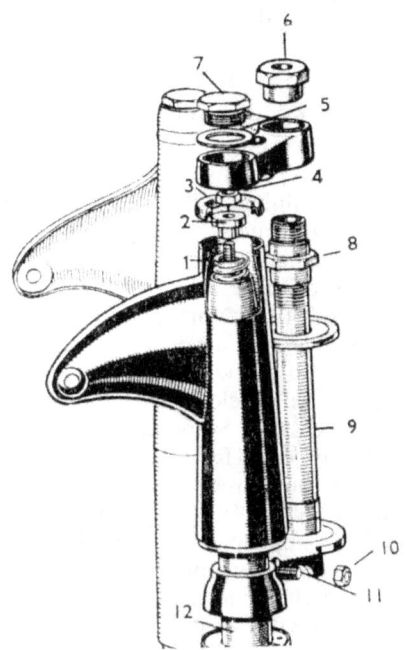

FIG. 54. UPPER PART OF 1964–5 "ROADHOLDER" FRONT FORKS PARTLY DISMANTLED AND THE STEERING HEAD ADJUSTMENT

1. Main spring.
2. Main spring locating bush.
3. Main tube top-cover ring.
4. Nut for top of damper rod.
5. Washer for filler plug 7.
6. Steering column and fork crown lock-nut.
7. Filler plug (near-side).
8. Sleeve adjuster-nut for eliminating slackness in the steering head bearings.
9. Steering column.
10. Pinch-stud nut for clamping main tube of near-side fork leg to fork-crown lug.
11. Pinch-stud for fork-crown lug.
12. Main tube of near-side fork leg.

provided in the standard tool kit) has the Part No. SPU1/49. The 1964–5 telescopic front forks differ from the 1959–63 type only in respect of width, and the damper and steering head design are identical to the 1959–63 type.

After eliminating bearing slackness in the steering head retighten the lock-nut on top of the steering column and again check that there is no bearing slackness and that the handlebars move freely. If the handlebars have been removed on a 1959–63 model, replace them. Finally retighten the two pinch-stud nuts which clamp the fork-leg main tubes to the fork crown, and replace the steering damper where fitted.

**Lubrication of Steering Head Bearings.** Keep both ball bearings well lubricated with grease in accordance with the advice given on page 27.

## FRONT AND REAR SUSPENSION

**The Norton "Roadholder" Front Forks.** Drain and renew the damping oil in each fork leg every 5,000 miles (1955–8 forks), or every 10,000 miles (1959–63 and 1964–5 forks). This maintenance is most important. Detailed instructions for draining and renewing the damping oil for the three types of front forks are given on pages 27–8. Never use damping oils of a type and grade differing from those recommended by Norton Motors Ltd. and specified on page 27.

The internal components of the Norton front-fork legs are designed for tough usage. Only after covering a very big mileage or if you ride very frequently over rough terrain is the action of the front suspension likely to deteriorate. If this happens a close inspection of the internal parts in each fork leg becomes necessary. Some parts may require renewal. This necessitates the draining of each fork leg, the removal of the complete telescopic-fork unit from the frame, and subsequent stripping down of the two legs. The removal of the fork unit is practicable by following the instructions in the maker's appropriate official Maintenance Manual, but the author recommends that the stripping down of the fork legs, inspection of the internal parts, and the renewal of worn parts be undertaken by the nearest Norton dealer or distributor handling Norton repairs.

**Girling Rear-suspension Units (1955 Onwards).** Girling rear-suspension units of well known and excellent design are fitted to all 1955 and later "swinging arm" models except certain 1956 and 1957 models which have Armstrong suspension-units fitted. The Girling units comprise telescopic tubes with totally-enclosed coil springs and an oil-damping system carefully set to provide really good suspension for the "Dominator" Nortons to which they are fitted. These proprietary units are sealed and there is therefore no risk of the oil damping-fluid leaking. No topping-up with fresh oil is necessary and *the units should never be interfered with*. It is, however, permissible to remove their top covers and grease the outside of the springs if the units become noisy while riding (*see* page 29).

If the Girling rear-suspension units become damaged or inefficient after a very big mileage it is usually necessary to remove them, after taking out the top and bottom pivot-bolts, and fit new ones. In the unlikely event of the Girling units losing their efficiency before a very big mileage has been covered, remove the units and take them to the nearest

Norton dealer or distributor for examination and the renewal of such internal parts as may be necessary. If stronger springs are needed after fitting a sidecar it is generally advisable to have them fitted by a specialist dealer. Special equipment is needed for changing the springs. Do not attempt to remove and fit springs yourself.

**Adjusting Girling Rear-suspension Units (1955 Onwards).** An external cam-ring adjuster for pre-loading the main spring is provided on every

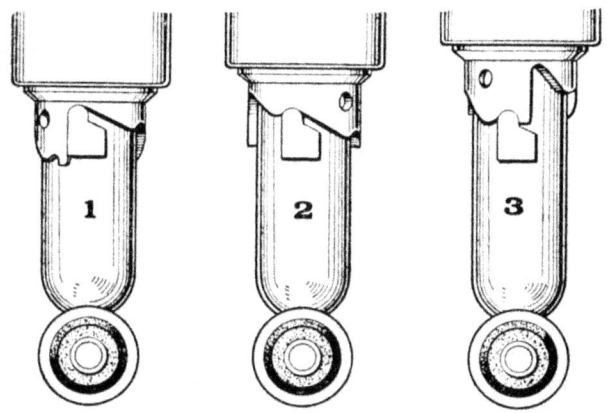

FIG. 55. THE THREE ALTERNATIVE SETTINGS OF THE CAM-RING ADJUSTER ON MOST GIRLING REAR-SUSPENSION UNITS

With the cam-ring turned to position 1 the minimum stiffness of springing is obtained. Turning it clockwise to position 3 provides the maximum stiffness of springing. Setting 2 gives an intermediate degree of springing stiffness, or pre-loading, obtained by raising the base of the main spring.

1957–65 Girling rear-suspension unit, but some 1955–6 units have no adjustment provided. The type of adjustment used is clearly shown in Fig. 55. On earlier models the shape of the cam-ring adjuster and the abutment below it varies somewhat, but the adjustment on all Girling units is similar and the cam-ring adjuster can be set to *three* alternative positions to suit variations in riding conditions and the load imposed on the motor-cycle.

Referring to Fig. 55, the normal solo adjustment (set by Norton Motors, Ltd.) is shown at (*1*). If your weight is above average or you ride your mount frequently over rough terrain, with the "C" spanner in the tool kit turn each cam-ring adjuster *clockwise* to the position shown at (*2*). If you carry a pillion passenger or heavy luggage, it is advisable to turn the cam-ring adjuster to the position shown at (*3*). Both cam-ring adjusters must, of course, be turned to the same position. The application of a little grease to the cam-ring adjuster will facilitate adjustment if any difficulty is experienced.

**To Adjust Armstrong Rear-suspension Units (1956–7).** Armstrong rear-suspension units where fitted instead of the Girling type (i.e. on some 1956 and 1957 models) require no topping-up or other maintenance. Each unit has a quick two-position adjustment for pre-loading the main spring to suit different riding conditions. The adjustment for normal solo riding by a person of average weight is such that the lobe of the adjuster sleeve is turned so that it does *not* rest on the cup provided at the bottom of the unit. This adjustment gives maximum movement of the shock-absorber springs.

Should you be above average weight, ride regularly over rough terrain, carry a heavy pillion passenger or luggage, or attach a sidecar, turn the lobe of the adjuster sleeve so that it *rests* on the cup. The lower spring cover on the Armstrong rear-suspension units is knurled to enable it to be turned by hand. No spanner is provided for adjustment, which should always be made with the rear wheel clear of the ground.

**The "Swinging Arm" (1955 Onwards).** The "swinging arm" or pivoted fork, has either "Silentbloc" or "Clayflex" bearings. In neither case is an adjustment provided, and no lubrication is necessary. Bearing renewal is not required until many thousands of miles have been covered.

# Index

ALTERNATOR, 34, 51, 52
Ammeter, 33

BATTERY—
  charging, 36
  leads, 38
  storage, 39
  terminals, 38
  topping-up, 36–7
Brakes, 104–7

CARBON deposits, removing, 71
Carburettor, Amal, 6–13
  cleaning, 9
  components, inspecting, 11
  dismantling, 9
  filter, 4
  float chamber, 11
  re-assembling, 11–13
  settings, 8
  slow-running adjustment, 6–7
Chains, 25, 91–4
Cleaning—
  chromium, 59
  distributor unit, 53
  enamelled parts, 58
  engine and gearbox, 59
  Lucas lamps, 42
  sparking plugs, 61–3
Clutch, adjustment, 97–9
  A.M.C., 98–9, 102–4
  Burman, 97–8, 99–102
Commutator and brushes, 31–2
Compensated voltage-control, 32–3
Contact-breaker—
  distributor unit, removing, 55
  gap, 53, 64
Control layout, 2, 3
Crankcase—
  breather, 20, 26
  filter, 17
Cylinder—
  block, removing, 73, 78
  head, removing, 69, 80

DIPPER switch, 29, 51
Dynamo maintenance, 30–2

ELECTROLYTE, specific gravity of, 39
Emergency starting, 51
Engine—
  lubrication, 14
  oils, suitable, 15
  removing, 90

FRONT forks, 27–8, 116
Fuel consumption, high, 8

GEARBOX—
  draining, 24
  overhaul, 104
  removal, 104
  topping-up, 24
Greases, suitable, 26
Gudgeon-pin removal, 74

HEADLAMPS, 40–3
Horns, 43
H.T. cables, 57, 66
Hydrometer, using, 39

IGNITION—
  coil, 52
  key, 50
  timing, 55, 87–9

LIGHTING, switch, 1, 43, 50
  system, 40–3
Lubrication—
  commutator, 21
  contact-breaker, 22–4
  dipper switch, 29
  dynamo and magneto bearings, 21
  front forks, 27–8
  gearbox, 24
  handlebar controls, 29
  magneto, 21

Lubrication (*contd.*)—
  overhead valve-gear, 17
  primary chain, 25
  rear-suspension units, 28
  rocker-arm pivot, 55
  saddle pivot, 29
  secondary chain, 25
  stands, 29
  speedometer-drive gearbox, 29
  steering head, 27
  wheel hubs, 29

MAGNETO—
  removal, 65
  rotating armature, 63
Major engine overhaul, 90

NEEDLE jet, 11

OIL—
  circulation, checking, 16
  control ring, 77
  pump, 15, 18
  pressure-release valve, 18
  tank, 16, 17
    filter, 17
Oil-bath chain case, 25, 95–7
Overhead rockers, 81–3

PETROL tank, removal of, 69, 80–1
Pilot jet obstructed, 8
Piston—
  rings, 74–7
  seizure, 5
Pistons, removing, 74, 78
Primary chain, 25, 91–2

RECTIFIER, 34
Repairs and spares, 58
Riding position, 1
Running-in, 4, 59

SECONDARY chain, 25, 92–3
Shorting, preventing, 30

Sidecar, fitting of, 112
Slow-running (*see* Carburettor
Snap connectors, 49
Sparking plugs, 60–1—
  gap, 61
  suitable types, 60
Speedometer light, 42
Starting up, 1
Steering-head adjustment, 114–16
Stopping engine, 3
Stop-tail lamp, 42
Suspension, 116–18
  Armstrong, 29, 118
  rear-suspension units, 28, 116–18
  "swinging-arm," 118

TAPPETS, 83
Theft, preventing, 3
Throttle valve, 11
Timing-control, automatic, 65
Timing—
  cover, 19, 84
  ignition, 55, 87–9
  sprockets and chains, 84–7
  valve, 90
Twist-grip adjustment, 13
Tyre pressures, 110

VALVE—
  clearances, 66–8
  guides, 84
  springs, 72
Valves—
  grinding-in, 72
  pitting of, 72
  removing, 70, 73

WHEEL—
  alignment, 112
  bearings, 107
  hubs, dismantling, 110
  removal, 107–10
Wiring—
  circuit, 44
  diagrams, 45–8, 56

# OTHER CLASSIC MOTORCYCLE MANUALS CURRENTLY AVAILABLE IN THIS SERIES:

## AJS (BOOK OF) ALL MODELS 1955-1965:
350cc & 500cc Singles ~ Models 16,16S,18, 18S

## ARIEL WORKSHOP MANUAL 1933-1951:
All single, twin & 4 cylinder models

## ARIEL (BOOK OF) MAINTENANCE & REPAIR MANUAL 1932-1939:
LF3, LF4, LG, NF3, NF4, NG, OG, VA, VA3, VA4, VB, VF3, VF4, VG, Red Hunter LH, NH, OH, VH & Square Four 4F, 4G, 4H

## BMW FACTORY WORKSHOP MANUAL R27, R28:
English, German, French and Spanish text

## BMW FACTORY WORKSHOP MANUAL R50, R50S, R60, R69S:
Also includes a supplement for the USA models: R50US, R60US, R69US.
English, German, French and Spanish text

## BSA PRE-WAR SINGLES & TWINS (BOOK OF) 1936-1939:
All Pre-War single & twin cylinder SV & OHV models through 1939
150cc, 250cc, 350cc, 500cc, 600cc, 750cc & 1,000cc

## BSA SINGLES (BOOK OF) 1945-1954:
OHV & SV 250cc, 350cc, 500cc & 600cc, Groups B, C & M

## BSA SINGLES (BOOK OF) 1955-1967:
B31, B32, B33, B34 and "Star" B40 & SS90

## BSA 250cc SINGLES (BOOK OF) 1954-1970:
B31, B32, B33, B34 and "Star" B40 & SS90

## BSA TWINS (BOOK OF) 1948-1962:
All 650cc & 500cc twins

## BSA TWINS (SECOND BOOK OF) 1962-1969:
All 650cc & 500cc, A50 & A65 OHV unit construction twins

## DUCATI OHC FACTORY WORKSHOP MANUAL:
160 Junior Monza, 250 Monza, 250 GT, 250 Mark 3, 250 Mach 1, 250 SCR & 350 Sebring

## HONDA 250 & 305cc FACTORY WORKSHOP MANUAL:
C.72 C.77 CS.72, CS.77, CB.72, CB.77 [HAWK]

## HONDA 125 & 150cc FACTORY WORKSHOP MANUAL:
C.92, CS.92, CB.92, C.95 & CA.95

## HONDA 90 (BOOK OF) ALL MODELS UP TO 1966:
All 90cc variations including the S90, CM90, C200, S65, Trail 90 & C65 models

**HONDA 50cc FACTORY WORKSHOP MANUAL:** C.100

**HONDA 50cc FACTORY WORKSHOP MANUAL:** C.110

**HONDA (BOOK OF) MAINTENANCE & REPAIR 1960-1966:**
50cc C.100, C.102, C.110 & C.114 ~ 125cc C.92 & CB.92
250cc C.72 & CB.72 ~ 305cc CB.77

**LAMBRETTA (BOOK OF) MAINTENANCE & REPAIR:**
125 & 150cc, all models up to 1958, except model "48".

**LAMBRETTA (SECOND BOOK OF) MAINTENANCE & REPAIR:**
125, 150, 175 & 200cc, all Li & TV models and derivates from 1958 to 1970.

**NORTON FACTORY TWIN CYLINDER WORKSHOP MANUAL 1957-1970:** *Lightweight Twins:* 250cc Jubilee, 350cc Navigator and 400cc Electra and the *Heavyweight Twins:* Model 77, 88, 88SS, 99, 99SS, Sports Special, Manxman, Mercury, Atlas, G15, P11, N15, Ranger (P11A).

**NORTON (BOOK OF) MAINTENANCE & REPAIR 1932-1939:**
All Pre-War SV, OHV and OHC models: 16H, 16I, 18, 19, 20, 50, 55, ES2, CJ, CSI, International 30 & 40

**SUZUKI 200 & 250cc FACTORY WORKSHOP MANUAL:**
250cc T20 [X-6 Hustler] ~ 200cc T200 [X-5 Invader & Sting Ray Scrambler]

**SUZUKI 250cc FACTORY WORKSHOP MANUAL:** 250cc ~ T10

**TRIUMPH (BOOK OF) MAINTENANCE & REPAIR 1935-1939:**
All Pre-War single & twin cylinder models: L2/1, 2/1, 2/5, 3/1, 3/2, 3/5, 5/1, 5/2, 5/3, 5/4, 5/5, 5/10, 6/1, Tiger 70, 80, 90 & 2H. Tiger 70C, 3S & 3H, Tiger 80C & 5H, Tiger 90C, 6S, 2HC & 3SC, 5T & 5S and T100

**TRIUMPH 1937-1951 WORKSHOP MANUAL (A. St. J. Masters):**
Covers rigid frame and sprung hub single cylinder SV & OHV and twin cylinder OHV pre-war, military, and post-war models

**TRIUMPH 1945-1955 FACTORY WORKSHOP MANUAL NO.11:**
Covers pre-unit, twin-cylinder rigid frame, sprung hub, swing-arm and 350cc, 500cc & 650cc.

**VELOCETTE (BOOK OF) MAINTENANCE & REPAIR:**
Covers LE Mk. I, II, & III, Valiant, Vogue, MOV, MAC, KSS, KTS, Viper, Venom & Thruxton. Includes some limited material on the Viceory scooter

**VESPA (BOOK OF) MAINTENANCE & REPAIR 1946-1959:**
All 125cc & 150cc models including 42/L2 & Gran Sport

**VINCENT WORKSHOP MANUAL 1935-1955:**
All Series A, B & C Models

~ WWW.VELOCEPRESS.COM ~

www.ingramcontent.com/pod-product-compliance
Lightning Source LLC
Chambersburg PA
CBHW070555170426
43201CB00012B/1854